Father and Son Journal: Just Between You and Me, Kid

INTERACTIVE PASS BACK AND FORTH BOOK TO BUILD STRONG BONDS AND MEMORIES

Copyright © 2024 BY START STORY HELPER INC.

All rights reserved. No part of this book may be used or reproduced in any manner whatsoever without written permission except in the case of brief quotations embodied in critical articles and reviews.

FIRST EDITION: 2024

Welcome to Your Dad and Son Journal! Get ready to embark on a journey that's uniquely yours!

HOW TO BEGIN YOUR JOURNEY

Start by creating a Time Capsule using the instructions on the following pages. This capsule will store all the keepsakes from your completed tasks in the journal. As you explore the journal, choose activities that resonate with you and your son at that moment. You can also build a habit of filling it out together daily.

WHAT EXERCISES ARE IN THE JOURNAL AND HOW TO APPROACH THEM

Dedicate 10-15 minutes of uninterrupted time for each activity. Some pages encourage reflection and conversation, while others invite you to play and use your artistic skills. These exercises are designed to engage your son and strengthen your bond.

 EMOTIONAL INTELLIGENCE DEVELOPMENT TASKS

Dad, if you encounter a task involving exploring emotions, make sure to be fully present with your son by putting away all distractions, such as your phone. This will help deepen the emotional connection between you. Take extra time to talk with each other and ask thoughtful questions. These tasks are perfect for finding peace and reflecting on feelings, especially after intense emotions. Watch your son's emotions transform into valuable lessons, laying the foundation for personal growth and positive thinking.

Consider writing notes in the margins about your insights and incorporating these practices into your daily life.

RELATIONSHIP-BUILDING AND SELF-AWARENESS TASKS

The same principles apply to tasks that enhance your relationship and promote introspection. Encourage your son to explore and express his inner world and values. Share your feelings with words of love, support, and gratitude. The journal will also guide you both in practicing politeness and responsibility and setting personal boundaries by reflecting on your interactions with important people in your lives. Establishing respectful behavior is crucial for family connections, making friends, and getting along with peers. Don't forget to write down valuable lessons, words of encouragement, and appreciation in the margins for your Son.

JOURNEY OF CONNECTION THROUGH GAMES AND CREATIVITY TASKS

Set aside specific time for playing games and crafting together. Use this opportunity to have fun and bond, or save these activities for later when you have more time. Gather tools like art supplies, pencils, and paper to create something together—painting, taking photos, or crafting. Be sure to put your small special projects into the Time Capsule Envelope. Make it a collaborative experience and celebrate each other's creativity.

 INTEGRATING MINDFULNESS

Mindfulness is essential for empathy and social interactions, helping sons build healthy relationships. The journal is designed to teach you to integrate reflective moments and activities into your daily life. For example, ask each other questions, give feedback, healthily deal with emotions, and offer affirmations. As you fill out the pages, you may find that certain mindful practices are especially enjoyable and helpful, potentially becoming a regular part of your routine. Remember, these simple acts are the magic behind connection and growth.

THE ONLY RULE: THERE ARE NO RULES!

This journal is full of inspiration and tools for you to enjoy. Use it in whatever way you wish—don't feel pressured to follow every entry. Feel free to modify, skip, or even create entirely new activities. The journal is yours to shape and adapt as you see fit.

MOST IMPORTANTLY, DON'T STRESS!

This is about taking small steps and focusing on the present. While some topics may seem overwhelming, you'll be surprised at what you can achieve by sharing your thoughts and emotions.

Let's check if you have everything you need to start the journal!

Art supplies:

- ☐ Pencils
- ☐ Paper
- ☐ Glue
- ☐ Scissors
- ☐ Free, uninterrupted time
- ☐ Inspiration
- ☐ A smile

NOW YOU'RE READY TO START YOUR ADVENTURE. TURN TO THE NEXT PAGE!

TIME CAPSULE ENVELOPE

Dad and Son, how about starting your journal with a fun DIY project? You'll make an envelope to store notes and doodles from your journal activities.

You'll need:
- Two pieces of A4 paper
- A ruler
- Glue
- Scissors

1.MEASURE AND CUT:

Use the ruler to measure and mark 4 cm (1,5 in) from the edge along the longer side of the first A4 sheet. This will be your cutting guideline.

2.TRIM THE PAPER:

Carefully cut along the marked line, removing the excess 4 cm (1,5 in) strip from the side of the paper to start shaping your envelope.

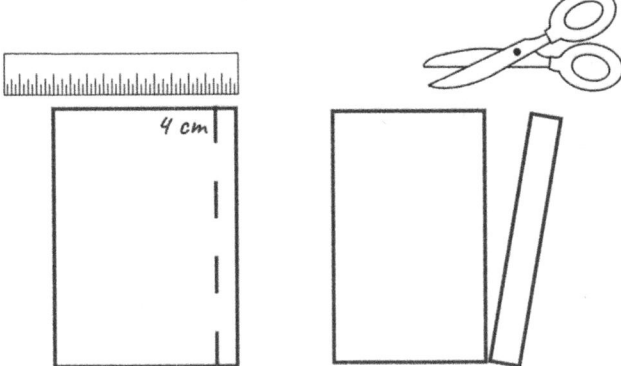

3.PREPARE THE SECOND SHEET:

Set the first sheet aside. Take the second sheet and measure 21 cm (8,.3 in) from the bottom. Mark it—this is your next cut line.

4. CUT AND FOLD:

Cut along the line you marked. On this trimmed sheet, mark 2 cm (0.8 in) from the right, left, and bottom edges. These will be your folding guides.

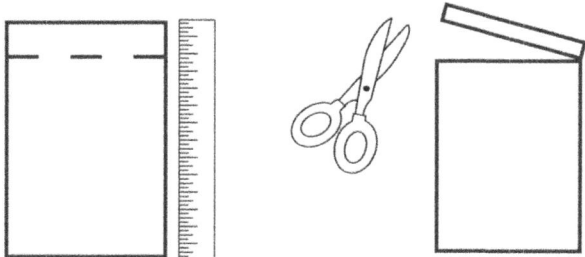

5. ASSEMBLE THE ENVELOPE:

Fold in the 2 cm (0.8 in) margins you just marked. These folds will form the inside of your envelope. Glue the folded edges of the second sheet. Then, press it onto the first sheet to join them, forming the main part of your envelope.

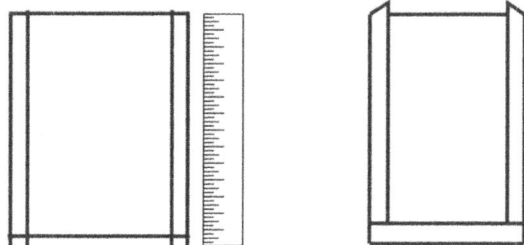

6. ATTACH THE ENVELOPE:

Fold down the top part of the envelope. Once it looks good, attach it to the endpaper of your journal.

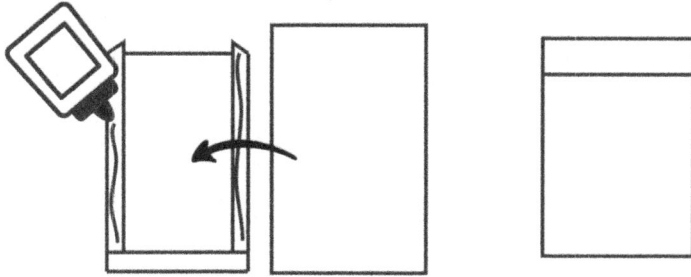

As you start filling up your journal, place fun notes or drawings into the envelope!

Our Story Starts Here

Paste your favorite photo of the two of you together right here!

Son, draw an awesome frame around the photo to make it even more special. You can use things that you both love, like superheroes, soccer balls, video game characters, or anything that reminds you of fun times together. You could also add elements that relate to the memory in the photo, like a beach scene if it's from a vacation or stars if it's from a night under the sky.

Today marks the start of our epic adventure together!
This journal will be our ultimate quest log, packed with thrilling activities, cool challenges, and unforgettable moments!

From now on, we will capture all the amazing things we see and do in this journal. Whether building something awesome, exploring new places, or having a blast, this book will be filled with our adventures!

Today's date is:
_____

This journal belongs to:
_____

and

_____

OUR PROMISE:

We promise to share all the fun, excitement, and laughter. With our imagination, creativity, and colorful markers, we'll create a treasure trove of memories that we'll look back on and smile about forever! Let's make every page an adventure!

Sports Wheel

Using this wheel, Son and Dad, explore various aspects of physical health and activity. Discuss your current participation in sports, exercise routines, and fitness activities. Talk about how the Sports Wheel can help you set goals and enhance your overall health.

Son

What sports are you currently playing, or are you interested in trying?
_____
_____

What do you enjoy about these sports?
_____
_____

Are there any new sports you'd like to explore?
_____
_____

How often do you exercise, and what activities do you do?
_____
_____
_____

What do you like or dislike about your current routine?
_____
_____
_____

Share the small, everyday habits that help keep you active and healthy.
_____
_____

Are there new habits you want to start, like drinking more water or stretching daily?
_____
_____
_____

Are you part of any sports clubs or community groups?
_____
_____

Would you like to join a specific sports club or try practicing a new sport? What sports club would you like to try?
_____
_____
_____

Dad

What sports did you enjoy playing the most when you were a kid? Why did you like them?
_____
_____

Can you share a favorite memory from playing sports during your childhood? What made it special?
_____
_____

Which sports or activities are you good at now? How did you become skilled in those areas?
_____
_____

What kind of exercise or fitness routine do you follow these days? How does it help you stay healthy and active?
_____
_____

Are there any new sports or activities you'd like to try? Why do they interest you?
_____
_____
_____

How do you stay involved in your son's sports life? What do you enjoy most about supporting him in his sports and activities?
_____
_____

Is there a sport you used to play that you'd like to practice again, maybe even together with your son?
_____
_____

DIY Pencil & Spoon Catapult

Materials Needed:
- 6 pencils
- 1 plastic spoon
- 2 elastic bands or hairbands (as shown in your photos)

Step 1: Attach the Spoon to the Lever
1. Take one pencil (this will be the catapult's arm or lever).
2. Place the spoon on top of the pencil, with the handle of the spoon aligned along the pencil.
3. Wrap an elastic band tightly around the spoon and pencil. This will secure the spoon to the pencil, creating the launching mechanism.

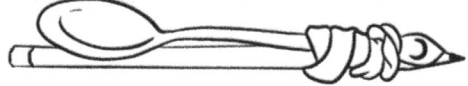

Step 2: Build the Base
1. Gather 4 pencils and align them side by side to form a stack.
2. Wrap an elastic band around one end of the pencil stack to secure them tightly together. This will serve as the base for your catapult.
3. Leave the other end of the stack open for now.

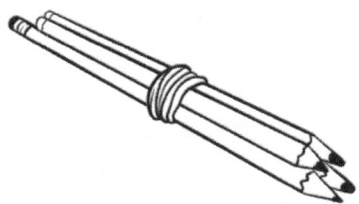

Step 3: Insert the Lever
1. Take the spoon-pencil lever and insert it between the 4 pencils in the stack. The spoon should be sticking out from one side, while the pencil lever sits between the pencils.
2. Ensure the spoon can pivot freely when pulled back, allowing it to function as the catapult arm.

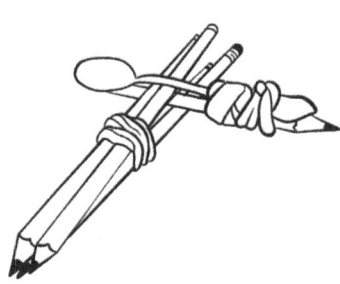

Step 4: Secure the Base
1. Once the lever is positioned correctly, wrap a second elastic band around the opposite end of the pencil stack to secure the pencils and hold everything together.
2. The lever (spoon-pencil) should still be able to move up and down smoothly, as it is not tightly bound by the elastic bands.

How to Play:
- Game 1: Distance Challenge: Take turns launching projectiles and measure the distance each one travels. The one that goes the farthest wins!
- Game 2: Target Practice: Set up targets like cups or a hula hoop on the ground. See who can land their projectile in or closest to the target.

How Does the Catapult Work?

When you pull down the spoon, you're building up energy like pulling back a slingshot. Letting go releases that energy, turning it into movement that makes the spoon snap up fast and send the object flying. The stack of pencils lets the spoon move up and down easily. When you press down on one end, the other end pops up quickly, using all that built-up energy to launch the object with lots of force!

Write a Story

Dad and Son, look at the comic strip about the act of friendship and support. You'll need to write the dialogues, taking turns with each other. What do you think is happening in these pictures? Don't forget to draw the last panel.

Friend in Need

1. Raccoon and Fox are playing together with an acorn, laughing and running around.

2. Wolf runs up to them, out of breath, and asks them to give him the acorn. Raccoon and Fox don't want to give it away, saying they found it first.

3. Wolf gets angry and yanks the acorn from Fox's hands.

4. Wolf starts running, but the acorn slips from his paws, and he trips and falls.

5. Wolf whining in pain and asking for help. Raccoon and Fox quickly run up to him.

6. Fox finds some medicinal herbs to ease the wolf's pain while Raccoon carefully bandages his injured paw.

7. Wolf thanks his friends for their help. He stands up, checking if everything is alright.

8. Son, draw the friends playing together. They happily toss the acorn to each other, laughing and enjoying their now larger group.

Heroic Rescue

1. The giraffe is reaching high up into a tall acacia tree, munching happily on some fresh leaves under the warm savanna sun.

2. The elephant approaching the giraffe with a friendly smile. The giraffe kindly plucks some leaves from the tree and drops them down to the elephant.

3. The elephant catching leaves with his trunk, and they enjoy the meal together.

4. The lion bursting from the tall grass, pouncing towards an unsuspecting giraffe with a fierce expression.

5. The giraffe is calling out for help, eyes wide with fear as he struggles to avoid Leo's attack.

6. The elephant charging towards the lion, trumpeting loudly and scaring the lion away from the giraffe with his imposing size.

7. Son, draw the giraffe and elephant stand side by side, smiling at each other with gratitude.

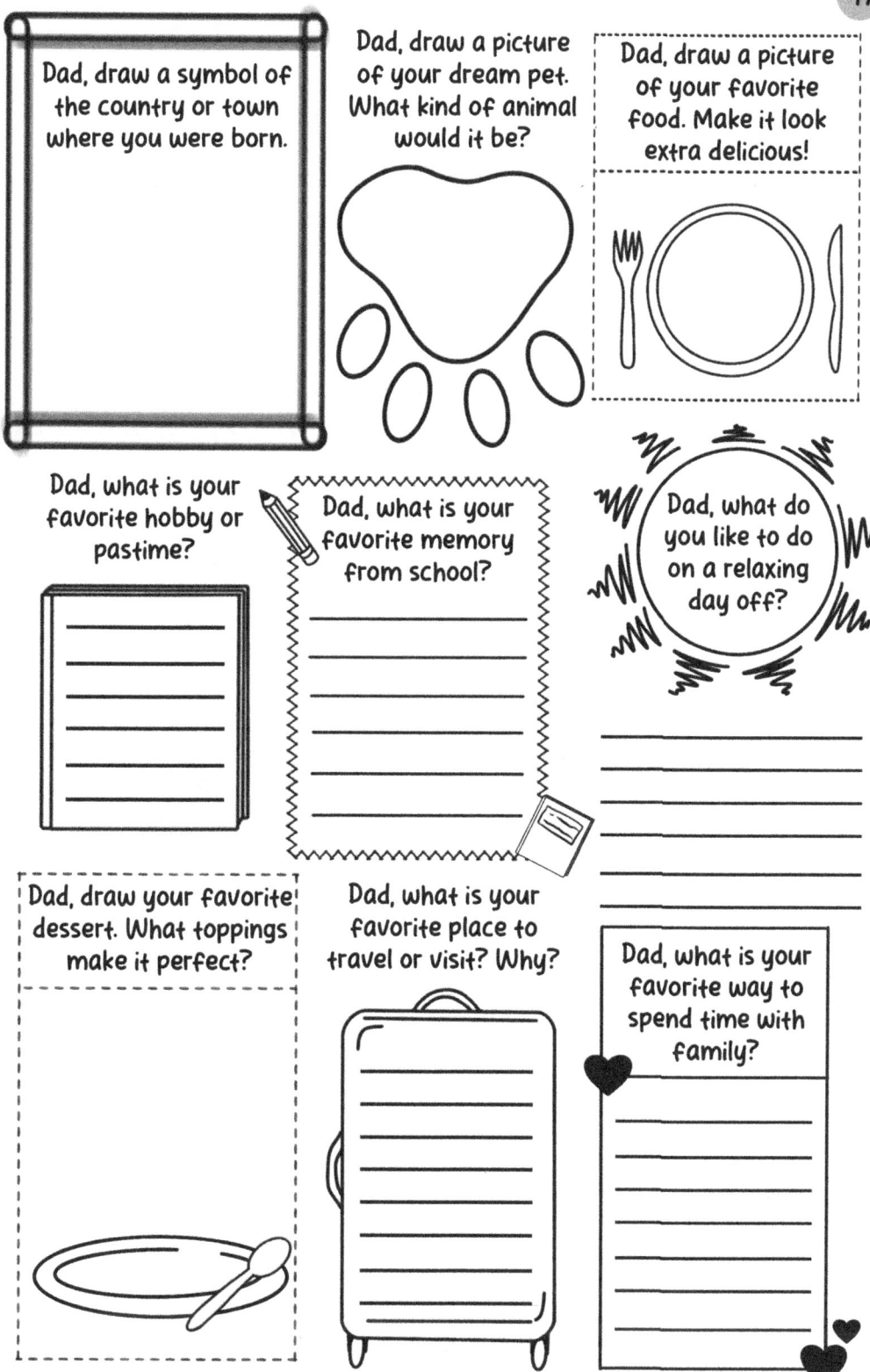

Leaf Animal Art Adventure!

Son, today, you and your dad will head outside on a mission to collect leaves that will bring the animals in your journal to life. Finish the drawings by attaching the leaves to the missing part of the animals. You can also cut the leaves into different shapes to match their features!

What You'll Need:
- Leaves of all shapes, sizes, and colors
- Glue
- Scissors for cutting leaf shapes
- A basket or bag to collect leaves

For Son

Hedgehog

Penguin

Squirrel

Bird

For Son

Mouse

Elephant

Fox

Donkey

Shooting Star

Son, take a moment to look at the shooting star. Write or draw a wish you have for this year. Think about something you truly hope will happen or achieve.

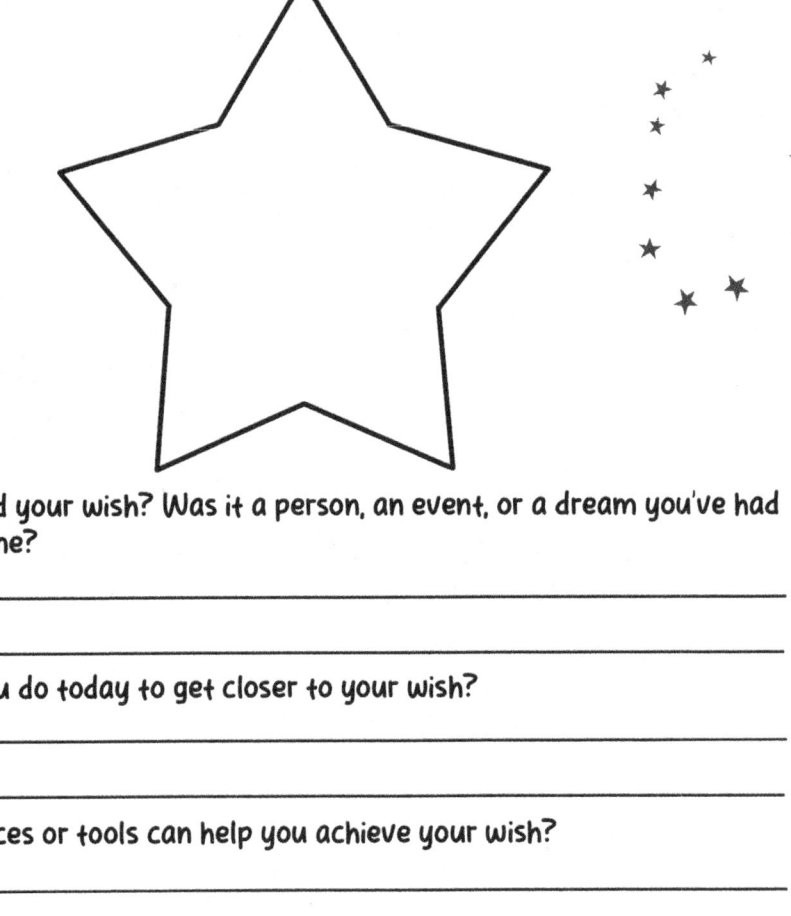

What inspired your wish? Was it a person, an event, or a dream you've had for a long time?
_____
_____

What can you do today to get closer to your wish?
_____
_____

What resources or tools can help you achieve your wish?
_____
_____

Together with Dad, make a simple plan for achieving your wishes. Write down the steps and any deadlines or goals. Check in with each other regularly to see how you're progressing.

_____
_____
_____
_____

Dad, take a moment to look at the shooting star. Write or draw a wish you have for this year. Think about something you truly hope will happen or achieve.

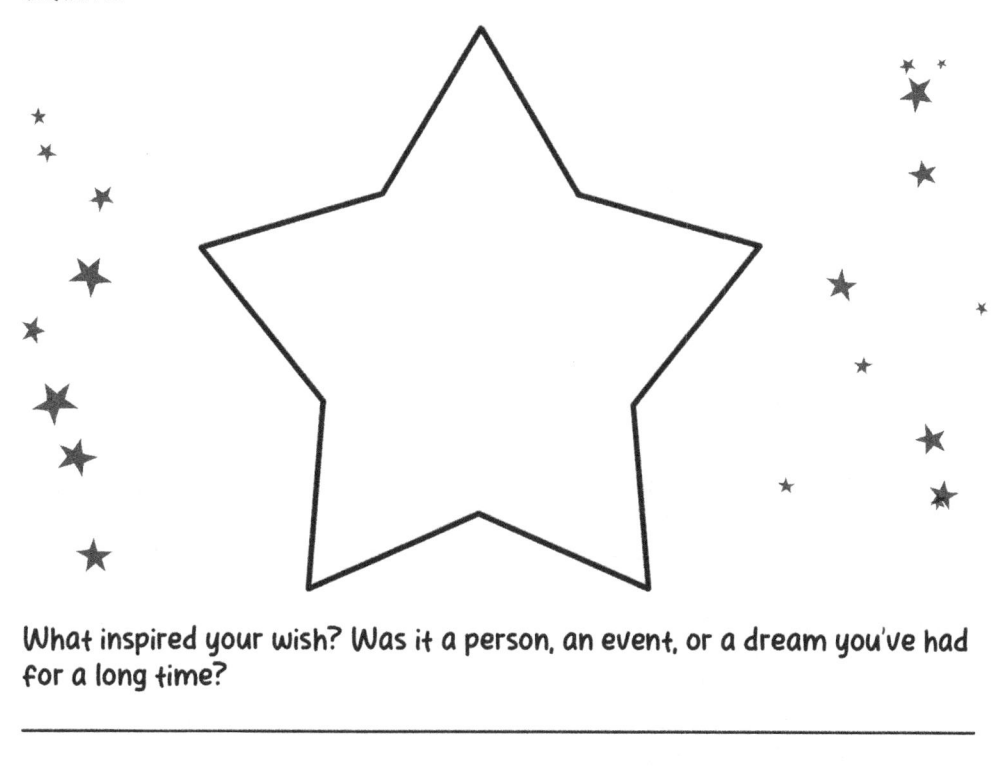

What inspired your wish? Was it a person, an event, or a dream you've had for a long time?
_____
_____

What can you do today to get closer to your wish?
_____
_____

What resources or tools can help you achieve your wish?
_____
_____

Together with Son, make a simple plan for achieving your wishes. Write down the steps and any deadlines or goals. Check in with each other regularly to see how you're progressing.
_____
_____
_____
_____

Snake of Activities

How to Start
1. Rock, Paper, Scissors: Begin the game by playing Rock, Paper, Scissors to decide who will be the first host. The winner becomes the host and prepares the tasks for the other player. Change the host after each activity.
2. Preparation: The host will set up each activity in advance, including hiding items, setting up obstacles, and preparing sounds or smells. Once everything is ready, the player can begin.

FLOOR IS LAVA

- The host sets up the room for "The Floor is Lava." Move from one end of the room to the other without touching the floor, using the cushions and chairs as safe spots.

SPY COURSE

- The host creates a "laser course" using string or yarn. Navigate through the course without touching the strings to retrieve a hidden "secret document" (a piece of paper) on the other side. Return the document safely to the host.

TREASURE HUNT

- The host hides a small treasure (like a treat or toy) somewhere in the house. The player follows a clue provided by the host to find the hidden treasure. The clue could be like, 'You're getting warmer!' or 'Colder!'

SOUND SAFARI

- The host creates different sounds using objects from around the house, like tapping on different surfaces or crinkling paper. The player closes their eyes and listens carefully, then guesses the source and location of each sound. You can extend this to include a "Smell Safari," where the host uses different scents (like spices or fruits) for the player to identify.

BUILD A FORT

- Work together to build a fort using blankets and pillows. Once it's done, spend a few minutes inside, sharing a story or imagining you're in a special place like a castle or spaceship.

SUPERHERO OBSTACLE COURSE

- The host sets up a specific obstacle course in the house. This might include crawling under a table, hopping on one foot between two chairs, or balancing a book on your head while walking a certain distance. The player completes the course while pretending to be a superhero on a mission.

GUESS THE OBJECT

- The host selects a few items and places them inside a bag or behind a curtain. The player reaches in (without looking) and tries to guess the object by touch alone.

FINISH LINE

- Final Challenge: Celebrate your journey by sharing one thing you enjoyed about the game and one thing you learned. End with a small treat or reward, like a snack or a fun activity of your choice.

The Treasure Hunt Blueprint

Welcome to the 'Explorer's Challenge'!
Son, today you're the master cartographer tasked with drawing the blueprint of your home. Start by sketching a simple outline of your house, including all the rooms, doors, and any special features you think are important. Once your blueprint is complete, it's time to hide the treasure! Dad, give your Son a few small items (like coins, toys, or treats) to hide around the house. Son, use your blueprint to decide where each treasure will be hidden. Mark an 'X' on the blueprint where you've hidden each item. Be creative with your hiding spots!

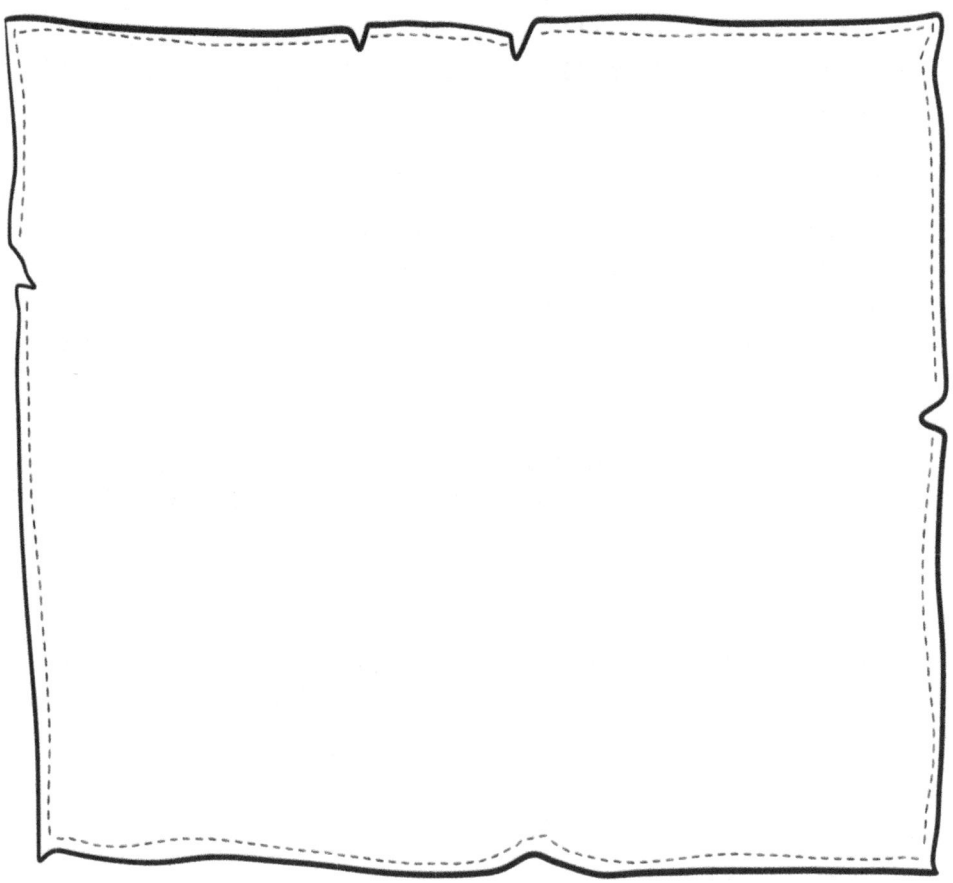

After all the treasures are found, it's time to switch roles! Dad, now it's your turn to draw a blueprint of the house and hide new treasures. Use a separate piece of paper to draw your version of the house layout, marking where you've hidden the treasures.

Building and Bonding

Dad and Son, it's time to decide on a cool project! Will you build a birdhouse, a model car, or maybe something completely different, like a superhero gadget that could solve a problem or make life more fun? Sit down together and discuss what interests you both. What project would be the most fun to build together?

_____

_____

Before diving into construction, you need a solid plan. Grab the A4 paper and sketch out your design. You can store the Blueprint in your Time Capsule envelope.
Here are some questions to guide you:

- What materials will we need for our project?

_____

- How will we divide the tasks? Who will be in charge of what?

_____

- What unique features can we add to make this project special?

_____

Now that you have your blueprint and materials, it's time to build! Work together, following your plan, but stay open to changes as you go.

	Son	Dad
What's the most fun part of the building process?	_____	_____
How do you overcome any challenges you face during construction?	_____	_____
How did you help each other during the process?	_____	_____
What's the next project you could build together?	_____	_____

Exploring Your Future with the Time Traveler's Machine

Son, let's talk about what you want to be when you grow up! Start by thinking about the things that excite you. Do you like working with technology, helping people, creating things, or being outdoors?

_____
_____
_____
_____
_____
_____

Dad, look at the collection of words your son wrote and brainstorm as many job titles as possible that match those interests. Write them all on the Time Wheel.

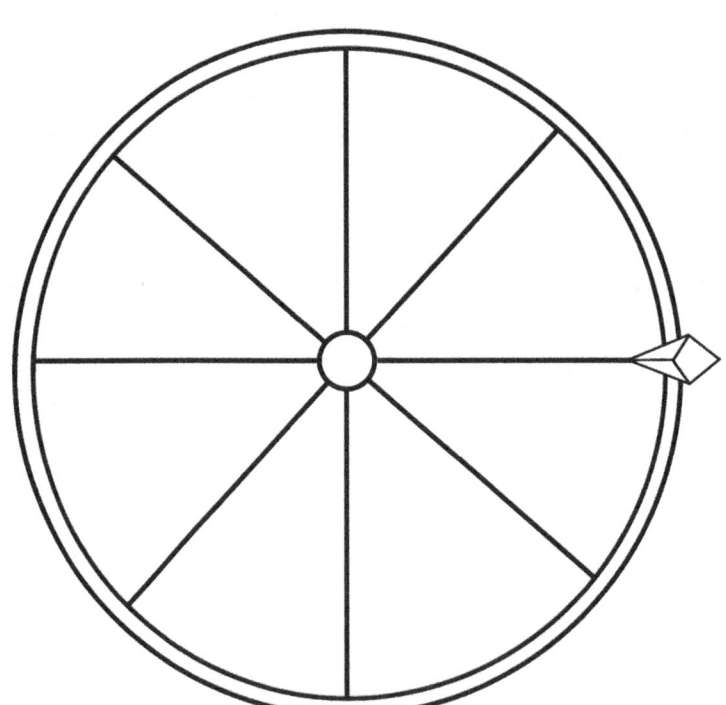

Now that you have a list of potential careers, it's time to journey into the future. Use the Time Traveler's Wheel to land a possible future job from your created list.

1. Son, place your index finger lightly on the outer edge of the Time Traveler's Wheel. Close your eyes or look away to avoid seeing where your finger is pointing.
2. Slowly move your finger around the edge of the wheel in a circular motion. Keep spinning your finger around the wheel as Dad watches and prepares to call out.
3. At a random moment, Dad will say, "Stop!"
4. As soon as Dad says "Stop," immediately stop moving your finger and see which career path your finger points to on the Time Traveler's Wheel.

Now that you've landed on a career, it's time to step into the shoes of that job and imagine what a day would look like. Here's how you can make it more interactive and fun:

Choose a role — will you be the person doing the job, or will Dad? Think about everyday situations that might happen in that career. For example, if you landed on 'doctor,' you could roleplay diagnosing a patient (Dad could pretend to be the patient, or you could use a stuffed animal).

If you have figurines or toys, set up a scene where your character performs the job. For example, if you're an 'engineer,' build a bridge or structure using blocks and have your figurines test it.

Son,
What would be the most fun or exciting part of your day in this job?
_____
_____
_____

Dad, what steps can your son take to prepare for a future in this field?
_____
_____
_____

Replay the game to get familiar with more career paths!

Balloon-Powered Car

Materials Needed:
- An empty plastic bottle
- Four bottle caps
- Two straws
- A balloon
- Tape
- Scissors
- A wooden skewer or a long stick

Steps:

1. Cut the straw in half and tape each half horizontally to the bottom of the empty bottle to serve as axles. Remember to remove the cap from the bottle first.

2. Ask your Dad to make small holes in the center of each bottle cap using a nail or a screw. Then, insert the wooden skewers into the bottle caps to create wheels. Congratulations, you've just made the wheels! Now, thread the wooden skewers with the attached wheels through the straws.

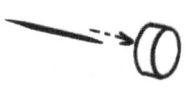

3. For better wheel adherence, apply glue to both ends of the straw halves. Then, thread the wooden skewers with the attached wheels through the straws. Allow it to set for 1 minute.

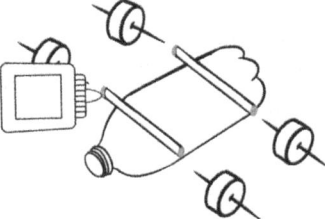

4. Attach a balloon to one end of a third straw using tape, making sure it's airtight.

5. Tape the balloon-straw assembly onto the bottle so the straw extends backward.

6. Blow up the balloon through the straw, place the car on a flat surface, and let go. Watch your balloon-powered car zoom away!

Experiment with different sizes of balloons or the weight of the car to see how it affects speed and distance.

Son, draw a picture of your car and describe how far it went.

Discover Your Town Together

Explore and map out your favorite spots in town together. Start by marking your home. This is the beginning of your adventure!

Father and Son, think about the unique places you love visiting together in your town. These could include:

- Your favorite playground
- The best place to eat together
- A fun entertainment spot (like a cinema, arcade, or park)
- Any other location that holds special memories for you both.

Draw a route connecting these favorite spots. Next to each location, add symbols or small pictures to represent what makes it special.

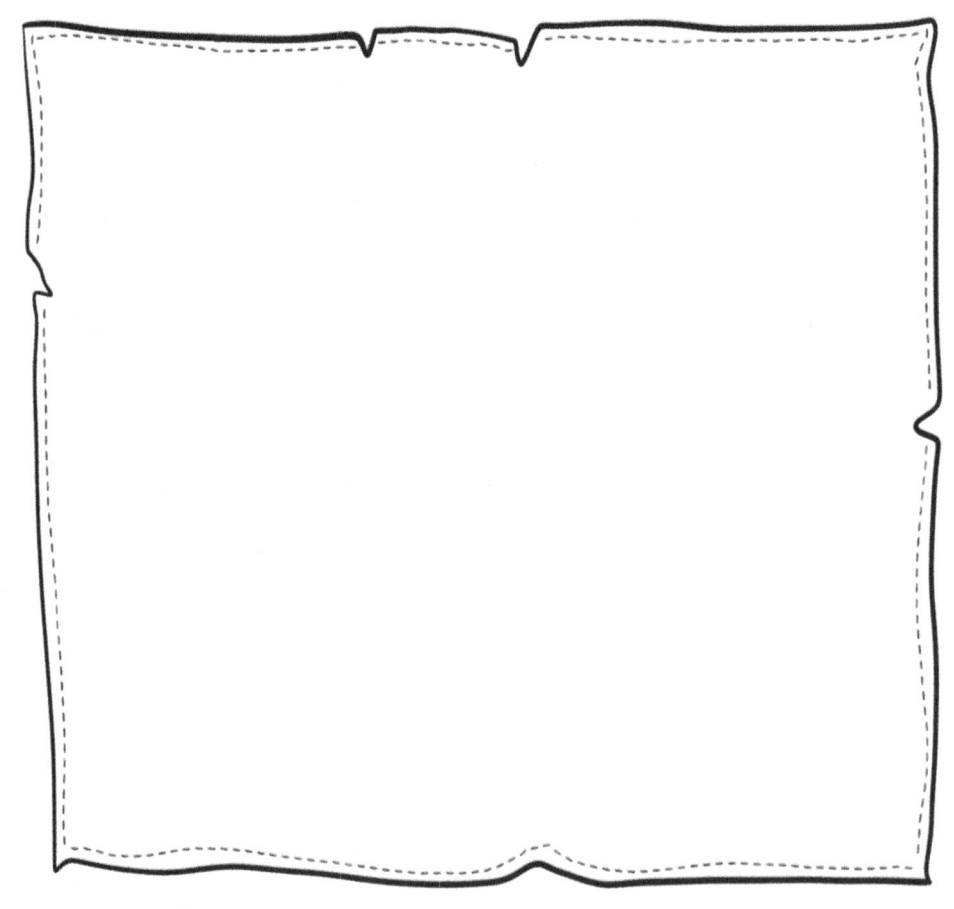

Describe what you do at each spot and why it's important for both of you.

For Son:
- I like to eat at _____ with my Father because _____

- I like to play at _____ with my Father because _____

- I like to train at _____ with my Father because _____

- I like to visit nature at _____ with my Father because _____

Use the space below to write any extra thoughts, ideas, or favorite memories. You can also plan future adventures here.

_____
_____
_____
_____

For Dad:
- I like to eat at _____ with my Son because _____

- I like to play at _____ with my Son because _____

- I like to train at _____ with my Son because _____

- I like to visit nature at _____ with my Son because _____

Use the space below to write down any extra thoughts, ideas, or favorite memories. You can also plan future adventures here.

_____
_____
_____
_____

Facing Fears Together

Every superhero has their strengths, but they also have weaknesses—things they are afraid of. The key to being a true hero is facing those fears.

For Son:
Draw your very own superhero costume. Think about what makes you strong and how your costume shows that strength.

Discuss with Dad what fear or challenge you faced. It can be a conflict with people in your life, dealing with strong emotions, or a nightmare. Fill in the gaps.

I am prepared to face my fear of _____
with my superpower of _____

For Dad:
Share Your Own Hero Journey
Think back to your childhood. What obstacles or fears did you face? Write down how you overcame them and what you achieved by taking reasonable risks.

_____
_____
_____
_____

Create a drawing of a special weapon or tool that could help your Son defeat his fears. Explain how it symbolizes strength and courage.

My Life Tree

Father and Son, imagine yourself as a tree. You start as a tiny seedling, but with time, you grow into a strong, towering tree. Your roots represent the support you receive from those who care about you, like your Dad. The trunk comprises the core values that give you strength—kindness, friendship, and honesty. These keep you steady and grounded. The branches are the dreams and qualities you wish to develop and grow as you reach for the sky.
Answer the questions and paint your tree in beautiful colors.

For Son

What kind of hero do you see yourself becoming?

_____
_____
_____
_____
_____

What values are important to you, such as kindness and friendship?

_____
_____
_____
_____

How do your Dad and other important people support you in your daily life, at school, and in your hobbies? _____

_____
_____

What super skills do you want to develop—whether it's being great at sports, excellent at school, or really kind to others?

_____
_____
_____

For Dad

What dreams and goals do you still aspire to achieve?
_____
_____

What new qualities or skills do you want to develop?
_____
_____

What values are most important to you?
_____
_____
_____
_____

How do these values keep you strong and steady?
_____
_____
_____
_____

How did your parents and other important people support you growing up?
_____
_____

What did they do to help you succeed and feel confident?
_____
_____

 # Changing rules

Son, have you ever wondered what living in a house with no rules would be like? Imagine waking up one day and finding no guidelines to follow—no bedtime, no mealtime, and no limits on screen time.
Write your no-rules list:

_____
_____
_____
_____
_____
_____
_____
_____
_____

Talk with Dad about what you imagined.
Dad, would things be easier or harder if things changed according to Son's rules?

_____
_____
_____

Would everyone be happy, or could there be problems?

_____
_____
_____

Dad, what rules are in your house?

_____
_____

Why do you think having those rules is important?

_____
_____
_____

Son, consider how rules help you feel safe, healthy, and happy. Write down a few reasons why having rules is beneficial.

_____
_____
_____
_____
_____
_____

Son, imagine if you could design one new rule for your family that would improve everyone's lives.
What would it be, and why?

_____
_____
_____
_____
_____
_____

Dad, imagine if you could design one new rule for your family to make life better for everyone.
What would it be, and why?

_____
_____
_____
_____
_____
_____

Emotional Weather Forecast

Explore your emotions by describing them as different types of weather.

For Son

Who and what makes you smile like the bright sun on a clear day?

_____
_____
_____
_____
_____
_____
_____

What has made you feel sad recently, like a cloudy day? How did you overcome that sadness?

_____
_____
_____
_____
_____
_____
_____

What irritates or makes you angry, like a sudden bolt of lightning?

_____
_____
_____
_____
_____
_____
_____

What makes you feel uncomfortable, like a chilly breeze?

_____
_____
_____
_____
_____
_____
_____

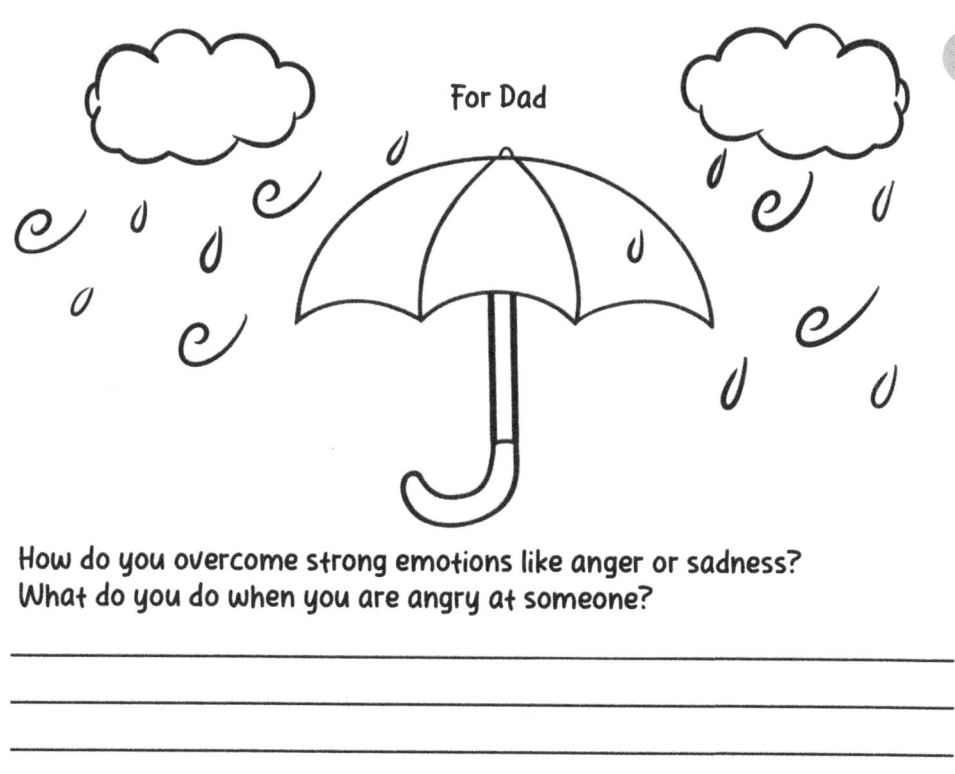

For Dad

How do you overcome strong emotions like anger or sadness? What do you do when you are angry at someone?

_____
_____
_____

How do you express sadness?

_____
_____
_____

Son and Dad, discuss these coping strategies and plan to use them the next time one of you feels overwhelmed:
- Taking deep breaths
- Talking to someone you trust
- Writing down your feelings
- Taking a break and doing something you enjoy
- Practicing mindfulness or meditation

Practice these techniques next time you feel overwhelmed, then come back later and write your observations.

_____
_____
_____
_____

Friendship Compass

Use your Friendship Compass to guide you in finding and keeping good friends. Reflect on the qualities and behaviors that point you towards strong, positive friendships and recognize the traits to avoid in others.

What are the good things your friends have done to you?

_____
_____
_____
_____

List the good qualities you seek in a friend.

_____
_____
_____
_____
_____
_____
_____

List the bad qualities you don't like in people.

_____
_____
_____
_____
_____
_____
_____

What behaviors make you feel distant or disconnected?

_____
_____
_____

Dad, write the warning signs that might show up early in a friendship that you should be cautious about—like someone who often puts others down or is only nice when they want something.
_____
_____
_____

What are the good things your friends do for you? What are you grateful for in your friendships?
_____
_____
_____

Dad, what's your favorite memory of you and your friends?
_____
_____
_____

Son, draw a picture or share a memory of your favorite moment with a friend or friends.

Son, keep your Friendship Compass in mind as you navigate friendships. Use it to help you make wise choices about who to befriend and how to build strong, positive relationships.

Paper Airplane Challenge

Objective:
Make and test paper airplanes to see which one flies the farthest or hits a target. Measure and score points based on distance and accuracy.

Things needed:
Paper (for making airplanes)
Tape measure or ruler
Open space (hallway, backyard, or park)
Pen and paper (for scorekeeping)
Hula hoop (optional for targets)

How to Make the Supreme Paper Airplane

1. Start with a Sheet of Paper:
   - Take a piece of paper and fold it in half lengthwise to create a center crease. Unfold the paper to lay it flat again.

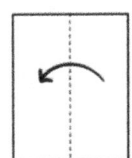

2. Create the Center Rectangle:
   - Fold the left and right edges of the paper towards the center line, aligning them with the crease to form a rectangle shape in the middle.

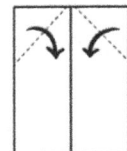

3. Form the Top Point:
   - Fold the top edge of the paper down to meet the center crease, creating a large triangle with a flat base.

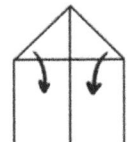

4. Narrow the Top Point:
   - Fold the top two corners inwards again towards the middle crease, making the top narrower and more pointed.

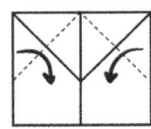

5. Fold the Top Flap:
   - Bring down the top point over the new folds, creating a smaller triangle that aligns with the edges of the rectangle below.

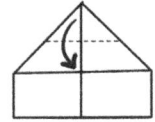

6. Prepare the Wings:
   - Fold the entire paper in half along the original center crease, with all previous folds on the outside.

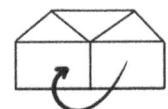

7. **Create the First Wing:**
   - From the folded edge, measure about two finger widths down, and fold the top layer outwards to form the first wing.

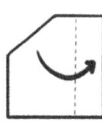

8. **Make the Second Wing:**
   - Flip the paper over and repeat the process on the other side, folding the opposite wing to match.

9. **Add Extra Gliding Support:**
   - Slightly unfold the wings, then fold up a small portion along the bottom of each wing to create stabilizers.

10. **Final Adjustments:**
    - Ensure the wings are even and adjust them to be slightly curved upwards for better gliding. Your Deluxe Glider Plane is ready to soar!

Setup:
   1. Create Your Paper Airplane:
      - Follow the instructions above to make your Supreme Paper Airplane.
   2. Find a High Spot:
      - Choose a spot to launch your airplanes from, such as a balcony, a small hill, or a chair. The higher the spot, the more distance you can potentially cover.

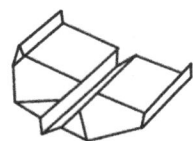

How to Play:

Game 1: Longest Flight Challenge
   - Take turns throwing airplanes.
   - Measure the distance of each flight.
   - The farthest plane wins!

Game 2: Target Practice
   - Place a hula hoop or other target on the ground.
   - Each player tries to throw their airplane through the target.
   - Move the target farther away to increase difficulty.

Game 3: Closest to the Target
   - Choose a target (like a cone or bucket).
   - Each player throws their plane towards it.
   - The plane closest to the target wins!

Reflecting on Memories with Dad

Consider Dad your first friend who's been with you from the start. Reflect on the special moments you've shared—times of laughter, lessons, and even disagreements.

For Son

What was the first sport Dad taught you?
_____
_____

How did you feel learning it together, and what did you enjoy most?
_____
_____

What was the first big achievement Dad celebrated with you?
_____
_____

How did you celebrate, and how did his support make you feel?
_____
_____

What was the first important lesson Dad taught you?
_____
_____

How has it helped you, and how did it change the way you think or act?
_____
_____

What was your first adventure together?
_____
_____

What made it special, and how did it bring you closer?
_____
_____

For Dad

What is the first thing you remember your son did that made you feel joy? Describe how it made you feel and why it was special.
_____
_____
_____

What was your son's first big achievement that made you feel proud?
_____
_____
_____

How did you celebrate this moment together?
_____
_____
_____

What was the first time your Son did something that surprised you in a good way?
_____
_____
_____

How did it change or deepen your understanding of who he is?
_____
_____
_____

What was the first time your son showed absolute independence?
_____
_____
_____

How did it make you feel, and how did you support him then?
_____
_____
_____

Ladder of Self-Esteem: Manifesting Your Strengths

Imagine your self-esteem as a ladder that you climb step by step. Each step represents a positive affirmation or quality that makes you feel confident and proud. Reflect on what helps you climb higher and how you overcome challenges.

For Son

What is a positive habit you have?

What makes you feel strong?

What is a talent or skill you have?

What friend are you?

What do other people notice that's good about you?

What is something you've done that made you feel accomplished?

How do you help others?

What do you love about your mind?

What are you smart in?

For Dad

Write down or think about an affirmation that helps you believe in yourself on each rung.

What is a positive habit you have?

What makes you feel strong?

What is a talent or skill you have?

What friend are you?

What do other people notice that's good about you?

What is something you've done that made you feel accomplished?

How do you help others?

What do you love about your mind?

What are you smart in?

Son and Dad, your positive traits shape who you are and help you grow into the best version of yourself. Keep these qualities close to your heart and remind yourself of them often.

Understanding Manhood

Dad, in your own words, what does it mean to be a man? Write down three qualities you think are important for a man to have.
___
___
___

Name someone in your life or from a story who shows these qualities. How do they show them?
___
___
___

Some people say that 'real men don't cry.' What do you think about that?
___
___
___

Write about a time when you felt sad or upset and how you dealt with it.
___
___
___

Why do you think it's important for men to show their emotions? How can showing emotions be a sign of strength?
___
___
___

What does being responsible mean to you? Write about your responsibilities at home, job, or with friends. How do you handle it?
___
___
___

Son, who is your favorite male character, and why do you like him?
_____
_____
_____
_____

What actions can you do to make you feel like your favorite character?
_____
_____
_____
_____

How can a good man show his feelings, like being sad, in a helpful way?
_____
_____
_____
_____

How can you be kind to people around you?
_____
_____
_____
_____

How can you have fun and still be responsible?
_____
_____
_____
_____

The Puzzle of Love: Exploring Our Bond

Imagine the special bond between you and your Dad is like a puzzle. Each piece of the puzzle represents something that makes your relationship strong and unique, like memories and fun times together. Let's work on this puzzle together!

For Son

- Son, can you think of a time when you trusted Dad to help you?
- What is something fun that you and Dad love to do together?
- Can you remember when your Dad cheered you up or helped you with a problem?
- What is something Dad says that makes you feel loved or happy?
- How do you know you can always count on Dad? Can you think of a time when he was there for you when it mattered?

For Dad

How do you support your son when he's having a tough day?
_____
_____
_____
_____

What little things do you do every day to show your son that you care about him?
_____
_____
_____
_____

How do you let your son know you're always there for him, no matter what?
_____
_____
_____
_____

What new experience or place do you want to explore with your son?
_____
_____
_____
_____

What makes you a proud Dad?
_____
_____
_____
_____

Learning from Dad

Son, imagine your mind is like a magical library full of books holding everything you've learned. Each book is a different experience, a skill, or a lesson. Let's explore this library together and discover what's inside!

What is one skill you've learned recently from Dad? Draw a picture or write about it in the book.

What activity would you like to try together with your Dad? Think of something exciting and new!

If you could choose any book to read with Dad, what would it be? Why?

What is a new topic or skill you'd like to learn about? How do you think Dad can help you with this?

After completing your books, share them with Dad.

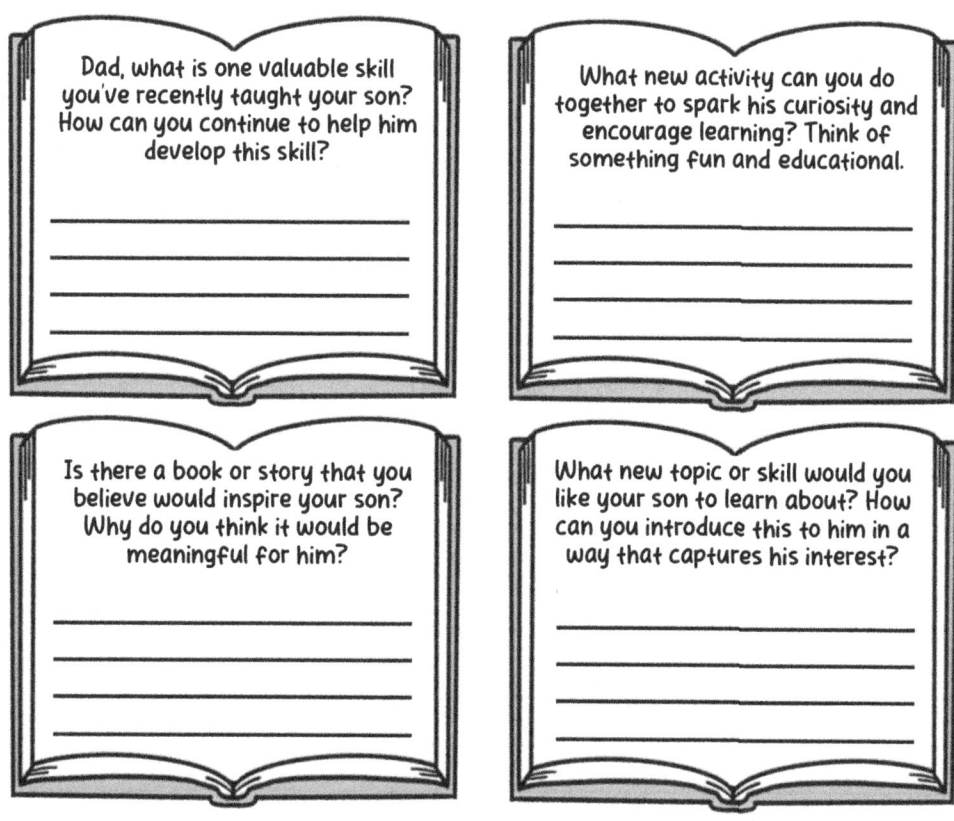

Dad, what is one valuable skill you've recently taught your son? How can you continue to help him develop this skill?

_____
_____
_____
_____

What new activity can you do together to spark his curiosity and encourage learning? Think of something fun and educational.

_____
_____
_____
_____

Is there a book or story that you believe would inspire your son? Why do you think it would be meaningful for him?

_____
_____
_____
_____

What new topic or skill would you like your son to learn about? How can you introduce this to him in a way that captures his interest?

_____
_____
_____
_____

After completing your books, share them with your son. Discuss what you've written and listen to his thoughts. Plan new activities and learning experiences together, making sure his library is filled with the knowledge and joy of shared experiences.

Create a Magical Story

Dad and Son, get ready to embark on a storytelling adventure! Take turns coming up with sentences to create a unique and magical story. Follow the prompts below to guide your storytelling journey.

Dad, where does your story take place? Describe the setting in detail.
_____
_____
_____
_____

Son, who are the main characters in your story, and what are they like?
_____
_____
_____
_____

Dad, what is the main problem or challenge that your characters face?
_____
_____
_____
_____

Son, what plan do the characters devise to solve the problem?
_____
_____
_____
_____

Dad, who helps the characters on their journey, and how do they meet?
_____
_____
_____
_____

Dad, how do the characters solve the problem and restore harmony?

___
___
___
___

Son, how do the characters celebrate their success, and what changes after the problem is solved?

___
___
___
___

Dad, what is the moral or lesson learned from the adventure?

___
___
___
___

If you enjoyed this activity, try it as often as you like! Follow the same questions, write the answers on a new paper, and store the story in your Time Capsule envelope. You can also add a plot twist—maybe the helper has a secret, or the characters discover something surprising. Introduce a new character later for more challenges or adventures. Most importantly, have fun with it!

Gratitude and Acts of Kindness

Son
Imagine you are a brave knight with a magical shield that grows stronger with every act of kindness and every time you feel grateful.

1. Color your shield: What does it look like? Add symbols or drawings that make it powerful.
2. Write outside the shield: Write down things or people you are grateful for. Each one makes your shield stronger!
3. Fill the village: Write the names of your family, friends, or people who are important to you in the houses. Your kindness protects them.
4. Write down acts of kindness you have done or plan to do for each of these "villagers." It could be helping with chores, saying thank you, sharing something special, or being a good friend.

Dad, you are a wise and noble king, ruling over a kingdom filled with love, joy, and peace.

Look at the village surrounding your castle. Each house represents someone important—your family members, friends, colleagues, and neighbors.
Write down the acts of kindness you have done or plan to do for each of these "villagers." This could include helping with daily tasks, listening when someone needs to talk, offering support, or sharing a kind word.

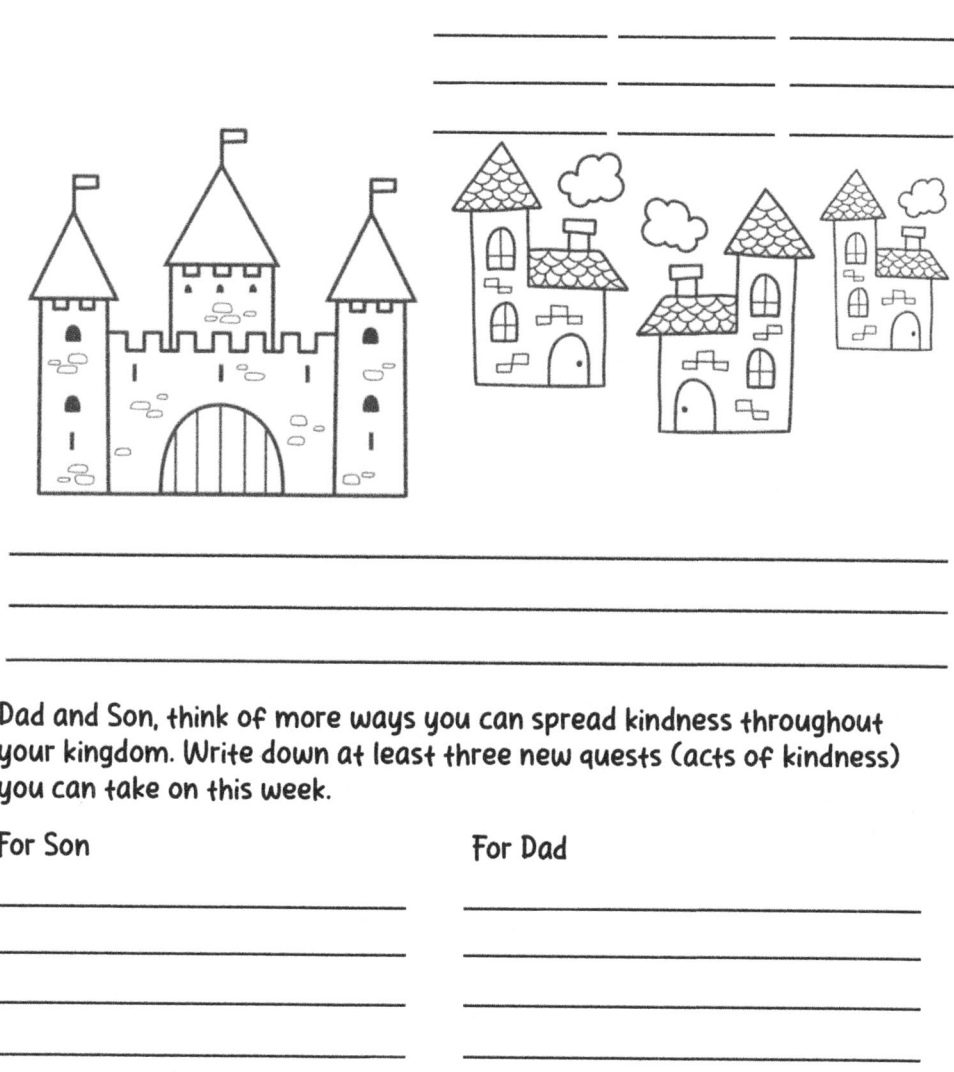

Dad and Son, think of more ways you can spread kindness throughout your kingdom. Write down at least three new quests (acts of kindness) you can take on this week.

For Son

For Dad

A Father-Son Teamwork Challenge

Imagine you and Dad need to find a way to cross a wide river. Working side by side, you will use your creativity and strength to find the best way across. Let's see how you can use your ideas and skills to safely make it to the other side!

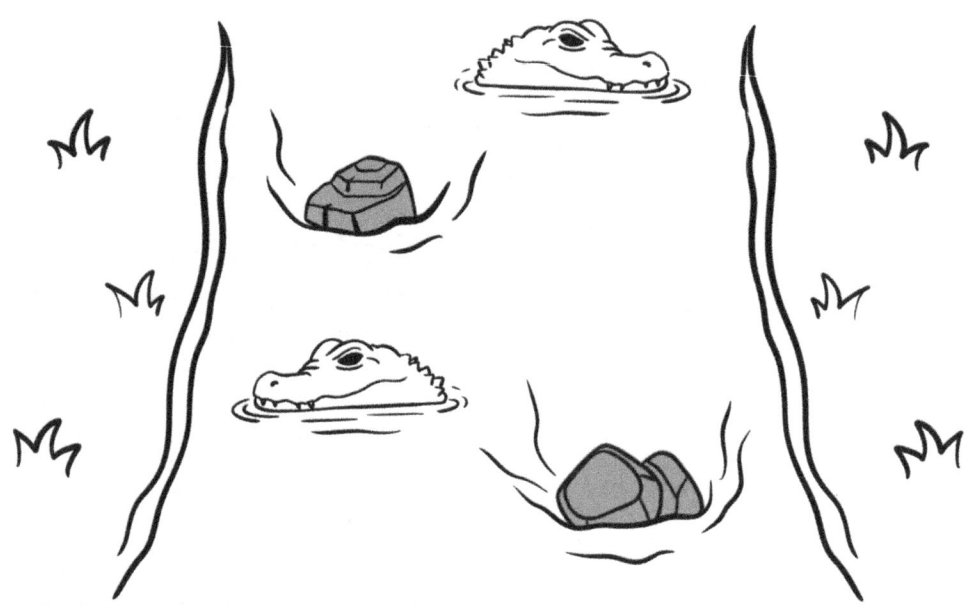

Son, think of different ways to cross the river. Be creative! What is your best idea for crossing the river safely?

_____

_____

Father, focus on overcoming the obstacles that might make crossing difficult. What challenges do you see, and how can you solve these problems to make the crossing safe?

_____

_____

Discuss your plan and refine it if necessary. Son, draw your final plan using the pre-drawn river picture. Consider your ideas and obstacles and show the safe way to cross. Use lines, symbols, or images to show how you and Dad will work together to get across.

 # Reflection Questions

What is more important in a discussion: defending your point of view or listening to others? Why?

Son	Dad

If this situation happened in real life, would you succeed? Why?

Son	Dad

What skills did you use to get to the other side? How did teamwork help you?

Son	Dad

The Race of Success

Son, draw a line extending from the start point to create your race track. You can make it loop around, wind through the page, or even spiral out. Along the track, draw several checkpoints where you will mark your achievements. Leave some space next to each checkpoint for writing.

As you draw each checkpoint, think about different achievements you've had. For each checkpoint, write or draw a symbol to represent an achievement. Here are some ideas:

- Checkpoint 1: Draw a trophy or medal for a sports achievement or winning a game. Write "I won..."
- Checkpoint 2: Draw a book that helped you learn something new or get a good grade. Write " I learned ..."
- Checkpoint 3: Draw a heart for making a new friend or helping someone. You can write " I made friends with...."
- Checkpoint 4: Draw a star for trying your best at something, even if it was hard. Write " I attempted...."

Dad, share how you supported your son and participated in his achievement. Talk about why it was important for you to be there and how you felt seeing your son succeed.

_____
_____
_____
_____
_____
_____
_____

Share your most significant life checkpoints and how they influenced your life.

_____
_____
_____
_____
_____
_____
_____

Responsibility Challenge Game

Each player (Dad and Son) creates daily responsibility tasks for the other. Complete the tasks throughout the week to earn points. The person with the most points at the end of the week wins!
Look at the table that has the days of the week (Monday to Sunday) already drawn. This will be your Responsibility Chart for the week.

For Son to Dad:
Son, think of daily tasks or responsibilities for Dad. These could be simple or fun, like "Help with dinner," "Read a story together," or "Tidy up the garage."
Write down one or two tasks for the Dad for each day of the week. Make them manageable or fun.

WEEKLY LIST

MONDAY	TUESDAY	WEDNESDAY	THURSDAY	FRIDAY
☐	☐	☐	☐	☐
☐	☐	☐	☐	☐
☐	☐	☐	☐	☐
☐	☐	☐	☐	☐
☐	☐	☐	☐	☐
☐	☐	☐	☐	☐

How many points has the Dad earned? _____

For Dad to Son: Dad thinks of daily tasks or responsibilities for the Son. These might include things like "Make your bed," "Finish homework," "Feed the pet," or "Help set the table."
Write down one or two tasks for the Son for each day of the week. Make them manageable or fun.

WEEKLY LIST

MONDAY	TUESDAY	WEDNESDAY	THURSDAY	FRIDAY
☐	☐	☐	☐	☐
☐	☐	☐	☐	☐
☐	☐	☐	☐	☐
☐	☐	☐	☐	☐
☐	☐	☐	☐	☐
☐	☐	☐	☐	☐

How many points has the Son earned?_____

Energizers and Drainers

Son,
In life, there are things that "fill our cup," making us feel happy, energized, and refreshed. These are the activities, people, and experiences that lift us. But there are also things that "drain us down," leaving us tired, stressed, or unhappy. It's important to recognize both so we can do more of what fills us up and manage what drains us.

Write down or draw the things that make you feel refreshed, happy, and energetic.

Write down or draw the things that make you feel tired, stressed, or sad.

Finally, consider and write down what you can do to replenish your energy when you're feeling drained.

_____

_____

_____

Dad,

Write down or draw the things that make you feel refreshed, happy, and energetic.

Write down or draw the things that make you feel tired, stressed, or sad.

Finally, think about and write down what you can do to refill your energy when you're feeling drained.

_____

_____

_____

Additional Question:
How can you help and support each other when feeling low and tired? Write down some ideas to show that you're there for each other.

For Son: _____

_____

For Dad: _____

_____

66 Get to Know Each Other Challenge

Use a game board to answer questions and complete challenges together, strengthening your bond and having fun. Pick a dice or make one from the template and start the game! If you land on a question, write an answer. Dad, pick a blue pencil to write, and Son, pick a red pencil! If you land on an action, you need to complete the task. If you've already been there, skip your turn. The game ends when one player reaches the "Finish" square. Take turns and have fun!

START	1. Describe your favorite toy and why you like it	2. A habit that sometimes annoys you	3. Go forward 2 steps!
4. How have you made someone smile recently?	5. What is one of your happiest memories about school? Write on paper and put in the Time Capsule	6. Draw a picture of your favorite animal and put it in the Time Capsule	7. Share a story about a time you felt proud of your success
8. Do 5 jumping jacks together	1. If you could travel back in time, which era would you visit and why?	2. What makes you laugh the most?	3. Describe your favorite place to visit and why
4. Reveal something you recently learned that you feel shy about admitting	5. Tell a joke and make the other person laugh	6. What do you like most about spending time together?	7. Step back 3 squares!
16. Share your favorite movie or TV show	17. Make an impression of your favorite character. Let the other player guess!	18. Share a fun fact you know.	19. What are you most grateful for today?

20. Describe something you're good at.	21. The best part about being a son or dad	22. A subject you enjoy learning about	23. Try to balance on one leg for 15 seconds.
24. Share what makes you feel loved.	25. A song that makes you happy	26. The last time you did something nice for someone	27. Do a silly walk for 30 seconds.
28. What's a talent you wish you had?	29. Pretend to be a superhero and strike a pose!	30. Your favorite food now	31. A nickname someone gave you
32. The best advice someone gave you	33. Step back 3 squares	34. A goal you're working toward	35. A movie you love watching together
36. A favorite outdoor activity	37. Write down a favorite memory from a family vacation on paper and put it in the Time Capsule.	38. Your favorite way to spend time on weekends	Finish!

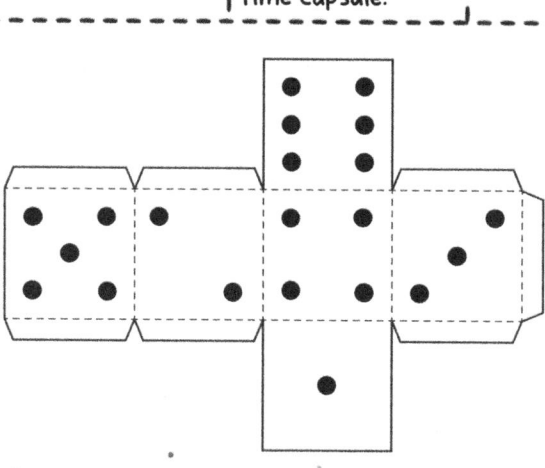

If you don't have a dice: Cut out a paper dice template and fold it into a cube, securing the ends with tape or glue. Decorate it with numbers or symbols to make it more personal!

Father and Son Bucket List

Work together to create a bucket list of adventures, experiences, and goals you both want to achieve. Use these categories to inspire your list and prioritize the ones that matter most to you.

What places do you want to visit and why? What would you like to see or do there?
Travel and Adventure Goals (countries, national parks, road trips, activity sights):

Son's ideas	Dad's ideas
_____	_____
_____	_____
_____	_____
_____	_____
_____	_____
_____	_____

Learning and Personal Growth Goals (books, clubs, workshops, events)

Son's ideas	Dad's ideas
_____	_____
_____	_____
_____	_____
_____	_____
_____	_____
_____	_____

Health and Fitness Goals (sports classes, games, racing, challenges)

Son's ideas	Dad's ideas
_____	_____
_____	_____
_____	_____
_____	_____
_____	_____
_____	_____

Creative and Artistic Goals (writing a story, crafting, taking photos, going to the concert or exhibition)

Son's ideas	Dad's ideas
_____	_____
_____	_____
_____	_____
_____	_____
_____	_____
_____	_____

Giving Back and Community Goals (volunteering, community clean-up, donation, helping around the house).

Son's ideas	Dad's ideas
_____	_____
_____	_____
_____	_____
_____	_____
_____	_____
_____	_____

Fun and Entertainment Goals (try new food, buy something new, visit the cinema, etc.)

Son's ideas	Dad's ideas
_____	_____
_____	_____
_____	_____
_____	_____
_____	_____
_____	_____

Talk about why you chose each goal. What does it mean to you? How will it make your lives better or more fulfilling? Choose one or two goals that you're both excited about starting work on right away. Father, plan to spend time together in your calendar.

Revisit your bucket list regularly. Update it with new goals, mark off completed ones, and reflect on your progress.

Stress Relief Toolbox

Son and Dad work together to create a personalized 'Stress Relief Toolbox' filled with tools (ideas, activities, or objects) that help you when you are feeling blue. Use this toolbox whenever you're feeling overwhelmed, need to relax, or want to have fun.

Materials Needed:
 1. A4 paper or cardstock (for a sturdier box)
 2. Scissors
 3. Glue or double-sided tape
 4. A ruler (for making straight folds)
 5. Optional: Decorative items like glitter, stickers, or markers for personalizing

Step-by-Step Instructions to Create a Box:

1. Transfer the template on the next page to A4 paper.
Place the journal under the A4 paper. Use a pencil to trace the outline of the template carefully onto the A4 paper. Ensure that you include all the solid lines for cutting and dashed lines for folding.

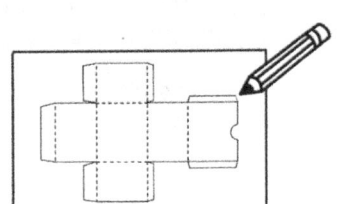

2. Cutting Out the Design: Once the design is fully transferred onto the A4 paper, use scissors to cut along the solid outer lines of the box template. Be precise to ensure the box folds and assembles correctly. Cut out any slots or notches that are part of the design.

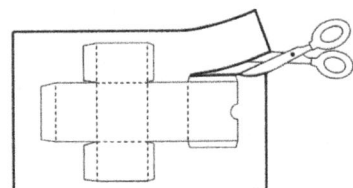

3. Use a ruler to help you score the dashed lines. Gently run the edge of scissors or a blunt knife along the ruler and over the dashed lines.

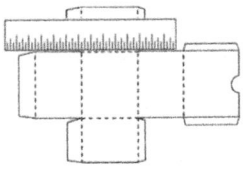

4. Fold along all the dashed lines. Make sure to create sharp, neat folds along the scored lines to form the shape of the box. Fold the tabs inward; these will be used to glue the box together.

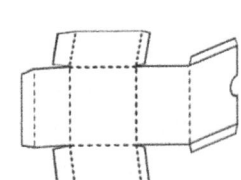

5. Apply glue to the tabs. Start folding the box into shape, aligning the edges carefully, and pressing the tabs to the corresponding sides to secure the box.

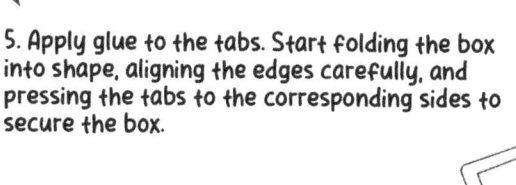
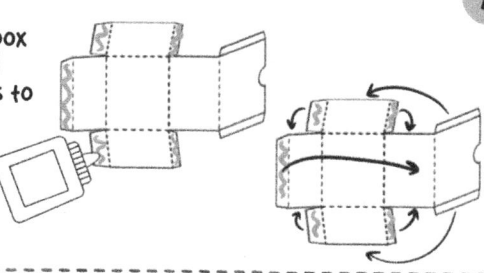

6. Add any extra decorative touches to personalize your box, such as stickers, glitter, or drawing additional festive patterns.

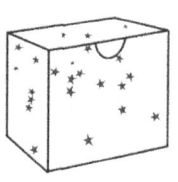

Sit down together and brainstorm activities, ideas, or objects that help you both relax and manage stress. Think about what makes you feel calm, happy, or recharged. It could be physical activities, creative activities, relaxation techniques, and comforting items. Write each idea on a small piece of paper or card.

Take turns sharing the tools you wrote down.
Example Discussion: "I put down 'drawing' because it helps me focus and relax. I feel calmer when I see the colors and create something new."

Place the cards in your toolbox. Make it a habit to check in with each other daily, weekly, or whenever you feel like it. Open the toolbox, pick a tool or activity, and do it together. Talk about how it makes you feel and if it helps.

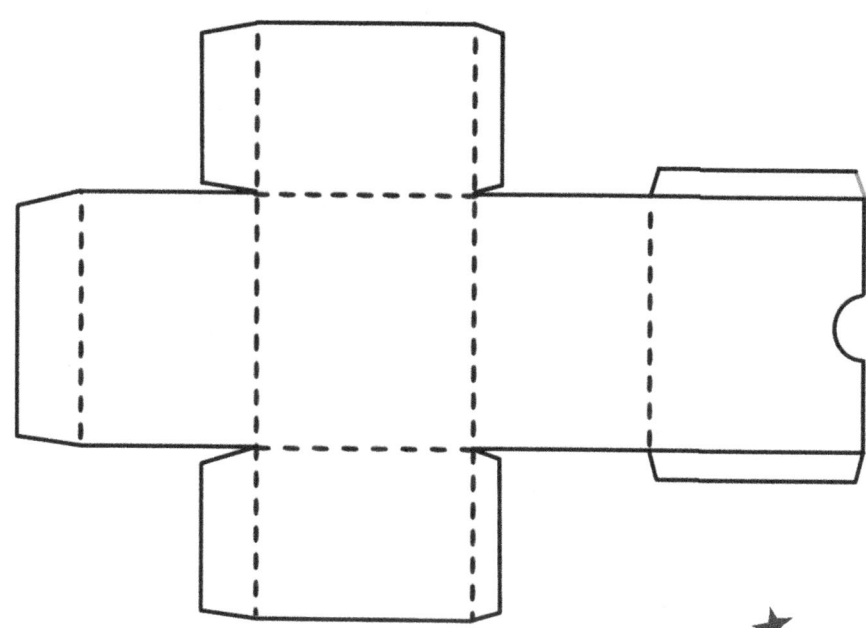

Saving Up for a Dream

Son, choose a big purchase you want to make. Write it here:
_____

_____

Write down the cost of this purchase.
_____

Son and Dad decide how to split the son's budget into different categories, such as earning money, saving, and cutting costs. This game will teach financial responsibility, smart spending, and creative ways to reach a savings goal.

Create categories for earning and saving. Write them in the left column. Examples may include gift, money and allowances.

Categories:	How much money will come from the category	Earned
_____	_____	_____
_____	_____	_____
_____	_____	_____
_____	_____	_____
_____	_____	_____
_____	_____	_____
_____	_____	_____
_____	_____	_____
_____	_____	_____
_____	_____	_____
_____	_____	_____

Son, which category will be the most challenging to earn money from? Why?
_____
_____

How can you use the budgeting skill that you learned in the future?
_____
_____

Shopping Budget Task

Father and Son, go on a shopping trip together. You can visit your grocery shop if you want. The objective is to create a budget for different food categories, make a shopping list, and then compare their planned budget to the actual cost of the items in their shopping cart. This task teaches budgeting, price comparison, and decision-making skills.

Before going to the store, sit down together and discuss the purpose of the shopping trip. Is it for a week's worth of groceries, ingredients for a special meal, or stocking up on essentials?

_____

_____

Divide the grocery items into different categories. For example, fruits and vegetables, meat and poultry etc. Agree on a total budget for the shopping trip (e.g., $50). Then, decide how much to allocate for each category based on needs and preferences. Write down the budget for each category.

Our budget is _____ .

Categories:	Category Budget	Actual Cost	Budget saved or exceeded
_____	_____	_____	_____
_____	_____	_____	_____
_____	_____	_____	_____
_____	_____	_____	_____
_____	_____	_____	_____
_____	_____	_____	_____

Total money spent: _____ Saved: _____

Take the list and budget breakdown with you to the store. As you shop, compare prices of different brands and sizes. Keep track of your spending as you put items in the cart. Once you're home, compare the budgeted amounts to the amounts paid for each category.

Dad, what changes can you make next time to improve your budgeting skills?

_____

Son, what did you learn about planning and sticking to a budget?

_____

Complete the comics

Dad and Son, look at the comic strip. It seems that the artist forgot to draw some of the panels. Could you help by drawing the missing images from the story below? It would be more fun if you took turns drawing each panel one by one.

Persistency is a key!

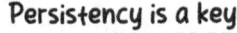

1. The forest was dark, and the moon hung high in the sky. A little fox searched for a place to sleep and found a small den on a hill.

2. The little fox decided to make the den bigger and began digging hard, moving dirt with her paws.

3. Son, draw the fox as he suddenly uncovers a strange locked treasure chest. Behind the chest, there's a long, dark tunnel leading further underground.

4. Dad, draw a map that was lying near the treasure chest.

5. Son, draw the fox walking through the underground tunnels, holding the map in her mouth, looking around to follow the directions.

6. Dad, draw the fox standing at a dead end in the tunnel, looking confused, as if she's unsure where to go next.

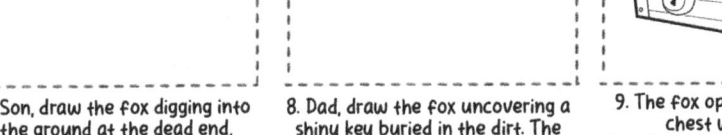

7. Son, draw the fox digging into the ground at the dead end, determined to find the key.

8. Dad, draw the fox uncovering a shiny key buried in the dirt. The fox looks excited and hopeful.

9. The fox opened the treasure chest with the key. Son, draw the treasure inside the chest.

Son, what do you think would have happened if the fox had turned away, disappointed when he hit that dead end?

Why do you think it's important to be persistent and not give up?

Act of Bravery

1. The cat is lounging comfortably on a cozy bed when the dog accidentally steps on the cat's tail as it walks by.

2. Son, draw the cat looking sad and hurt, its ears back and eyes looking down.

3. Dad, draw the the dog coming back into the room with a toy mouse in its mouth.

4. Son, draw as the dog places the toy mouse in front of the cat, wagging its tail, trying to cheer up the cat.

5. Dad, draw the toy mouse suddenly starting to move on its own! The dog looks surprised, barking loudly.

6. Son, draw the dog chasing after the moving toy mouse, barking and trying to catch it. The toy mouse is zipping around the room, knocking on things.

7. Dad, draw the dog, finally managing to corner the toy mouse and flipping it over with its paw. The toy mouse makes a whirring sound and then stops moving, turning off.

8. Son, draw the dog standing proudly over the flipped toy mouse, panting but looking victorious. The cat peeks out from behind the pillow, still a bit wary but relieved.

9. The dog stands next to the cat, wagging its tail, both of them realizing the mouse was just a toy. They share a look, and the cat lets out a small, amused purr, feeling more at ease.

Son, how did the dog make amends with the cat?

What do you think is the best way to apologize if you do something wrong?

Time Management Bingo

Rules for each player:

Look at the 5x5 bingo grid. Each square represents a different task or activity. Your opponent will write down tasks in the squares for you (e.g., "Read a story," "Do a quick exercise," "Clean a drawer," "Call a friend," "Draw a picture," "Help with laundry").

Set Time Limits: Once the tasks are written down, assign a reasonable time limit for each activity (e.g., 5-20 minutes). This will challenge you to complete each task within the set time.

Complete the Tasks: Start completing the tasks on your bingo card. Use a timer to ensure you stay within the time limit for each activity. Mark a square when you complete a task within the time limit.

Aim for a Bingo: The goal is to complete a line of tasks either horizontally, vertically, or diagonally on your bingo card. Each completed line earns a small reward, such as a favorite treat, extra playtime, or choosing a family activity.

Son's Bingo

		Free		

Dad's Bingo

		Free		

What did you learn about managing your time from playing this game? Was it enough time for you to finish tasks in time?

Son

_____
_____
_____
_____
_____

Dad

_____
_____
_____
_____
_____

How can you apply what you learned to your daily routine?

Son

_____
_____
_____
_____
_____

Dad

_____
_____
_____
_____
_____

Father and Son Athletic Challenge

To test your physical abilities and set new fitness goals together! Use this fun and engaging challenge to improve your athletic skills while spending quality time with each other.

Remember, try not to compete with each other. Instead, try to improve your results.

    Materials Needed:
- A stopwatch or phone timer
- Measuring tape or a marked area for distances
- A ball for throwing
- A safe area for jumping, running, and performing exercises

Challenge Tasks:

100-Meter Dash:
Task: Run 100 meters as fast as you can. Goal: Work on speed and aim to beat your own times.

	1st try	2nd try	3rd try
Dad Results:	____	____	____
Son's Results:	____	____	____

Sit-Up Challenge:
Task: Do as many sit-ups as you can in one go. Goal: Increase the number of sit-ups each time you try.

	1st try	2nd try	3rd try
Dad Results:	____	____	____
Son's Results:	____	____	____

Long Jump:
Task: Stand with both feet together and see how far you can jump forward. Measure the distance in feet or meters. Goal: Practice jumping techniques to improve your distance.

	1st try	2nd try	3rd try
Dad Results:	____	____	____
Son's Results:	____	____	____

Throwing Challenge:
Task: Use a ball and see how far you can throw it. Record the distance of the throw. Goal: Try different throwing techniques to increase your distance.

	1st try	2nd try	3rd try
Dad Results:	____	____	____
Son's Results:	____	____	____

Push-Up Challenge:
Task: Do as many push-ups as you can without stopping.
Goal: Increase the number of push-ups each time you try.

	1st try	2nd try	3rd try
Dad Results:	_____	_____	_____
Son's Results:	_____	_____	_____

Plank Hold Challenge:
Task: Hold a plank position for as long as possible.
Goal: Increase the time you can hold the plank with each attempt.

	1st try	2nd try	3rd try
Dad Results:	_____	_____	_____
Son's Results:	_____	_____	_____

Jump Rope Challenge:
Task: Use a jump rope and see how many jumps you can complete without stopping.
Goal: Increase the number of jumps each time you try.

	1st try	2nd try	3rd try
Dad Results:	_____	_____	_____
Son's Results:	_____	_____	_____

Discuss your personal athletic goals together. What would you each like to improve on?

Son:	Dad:
_____	_____
_____	_____
_____	_____
_____	_____

Create a plan on how you will train to reach them.
_____
_____
_____

Prepare for the Life's Obstacles with the Adventure Map

Dad and Son, you are bold adventurers on a mission to unlock a mystery. Along the path, you will face 4 unique monsters that will test your teamwork. Answer the questions together to move forward. Once you reach the treasure, you'll uncover the secret word for success!

Son, how do you feel when you're facing something difficult?	Dad, how do you help your son build courage and stay calm in tough situations?

Son, what is something you've learned from dad that you'll always remember?	Dad, how do you guide your son in learning important life lessons?

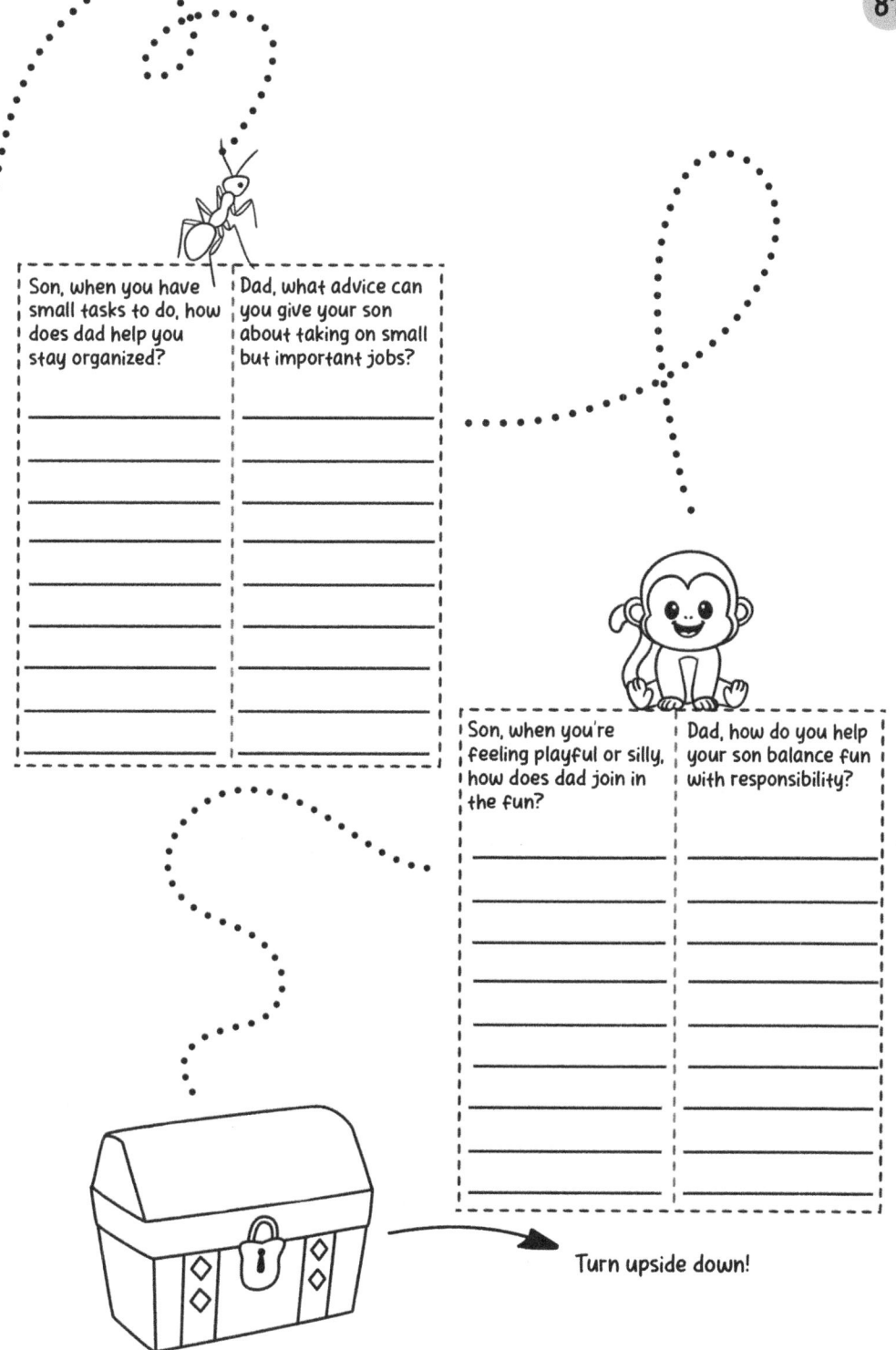

Son, when you have small tasks to do, how does dad help you stay organized?

Dad, what advice can you give your son about taking on small but important jobs?

Son, when you're feeling playful or silly, how does dad join in the fun?

Dad, how do you help your son balance fun with responsibility?

Turn upside down!

To uncover the mystery of success, combine the first letters of the animals' names.

Family Trivia Game

Dad and Son, let's see who knows each other best! Grab a piece of paper to write down your guesses.
Dad, you'll ask the questions and write the correct answers in your journal, but don't show them to your Son.
Son, you'll write down your guesses on your paper. No peeking at Dad's journal!

	Son's Guess	Correct Answer	Did he get it right?
What is Dad's favorite type of music to listen to while driving?			☐
What is Dad's favorite thing to do on a Sunday afternoon?			☐
If Dad could have any vehicle, what would it be?			☐
What is Dad's favorite way to celebrate his birthday?			☐
What is Dad's least favorite chore around the house?			☐
What is Dad's favorite type of weather and why?			☐
What is Dad's favorite way to exercise or stay active?			☐
What's one creative project Dad is really proud of?			☐
What is Dad's favorite type of adventure (e.g., hiking, road trips, exploring new cities)?			☐
What's Dad's favorite holiday?			☐

How many did Son get right? _____

Now it's your turn, Son! You ask the questions and write the correct answers in your journal. Don't show your answers to Dad yet.
Dad, write down your guesses on your paper. No peeking at Son's journal!

	Dad's Guess	Correct Answer	Did he get it right?
What is your Son's favorite thing to do at school and why?			☐
What is your Son's dream vacation destination?			☐
What's your Son's favorite activity to do with his friends?			☐
If your Son could have any job in the world, what would it be?			☐
What is your Son's favorite snack to eat while watching a movie?			☐
If your Son had a lot of money, what's the first thing he would buy?			☐
What is your Son's favorite thing to learn about?			☐
What's the bravest thing your Son has ever done?			☐
What is your Son's favorite type of weather and why?			☐
What's your Son's favorite way to spend time with you?			☐

How many did Dad get right? _____

Would You Rather

Son, ready for some fun? Grab your pens and get ready to dive into these choices. There are two columns: one for Dad and one for you. Take turns answering each question and write your answers in the columns. After you've both answered all the questions, it's time for the best part—talk about why you chose what you did! See if you can guess each other's answers before you write them down, and have a laugh comparing your choices!

Question	Dad's Answer	Son's Answer
1. Would you rather travel back in time to the year your parents were born or travel 20 years into the future?		
2. Would you rather surf a 100-foot wave or scuba dive 100 feet under the ocean?		
3. Would you always want to be 30 minutes early or 15 minutes late for everything?		
4. Would you choose to have a personal robot that cooks whatever you want or one that does all your chores?		
5. Would you rather have 10 siblings or no siblings?		
6. Would you rather move every year or live in the same town forever?		
7. Would you prefer taking only cold showers for the rest of your life or only being able to drink hot water?		
8. Would you rather stay overnight in a tree house or submarine?		
9. Would you rather attend the Super Bowl or meet your favorite football player in person?		
10. Would you rather have a dog that only meows or a cat that only barks?		
11. Would you rather give up wearing pants or give up wearing shorts forever?		
12. Would you prefer to get a million dollars right now or receive a hundred dollars every day forever?		
13. Would you choose to work at your dream job but make only a little money, or do a job you dislike but make a lot of money?		

Question	Dad's Answer	Son's Answer

14. Would you rather be stranded on a desert island for a week or stuck in a packed elevator for a day?

15. Would you rather give up Christmas or your birthday celebration?

16. Would you rather have superhuman speed or superhuman strength?

17. Would you rather be able to communicate with every animal or speak every human language?

18. Would you choose to be a police officer or a firefighter?

19. Would you rather sneeze confetti or cough bubbles?

20. Would you rather be able to read minds or be invisible?

21. Would you prefer to have wings like a bird and be able to fly or fins like a fish and breathe underwater?

22. Would you rather eat pizza for every meal for a whole year or never eat pizza again?

23. Would you rather be able to time travel to any moment in history or be able to visit any planet in the universe?

24. Would you choose to be famous for being a brilliant scientist or a popular artist?

25. Would you prefer to have a magic carpet that can fly or a crystal ball that shows the future?

26. Would you choose to have the power to control the weather or the ability to talk to plants and make them grow?

27. Would you choose to live in a world where it's always winter or a world where it's always summer?

28. Would you prefer to be able to control fire or control water with your hands?

29. Would you choose to be a famous athlete who wins every competition or a famous inventor who creates incredible gadgets?

30. Would you rather have your own personal spaceship or a huge castle surrounded by enchanted forests?

My Big Family

_____
_____

Son, choose a favorite family photo that includes everyone or draw your family from memory.
Use the space provided to write the name of each person.

What is your favorite memory with each person? Describe the moment and why it stands out to you. What are some fun or interesting facts about this person?

Name	Memory	Interesting Fact
_____	_____	_____
_____	_____	_____
_____	_____	_____
_____	_____	_____

Dad, what is your favorite memory with each person? Describe the moment and why it stands out to you. What are some fun or interesting facts about this person?

Name	Memory	Interesting Fact

Dad and Son, plan a family gathering together. Choose a date, theme, and place. Put it in your calendar, and a reminder to prepare for the event.
Write down your impression of hosting a family event.

For Son: _____
_____
_____
_____
_____

For Dad: _____
_____
_____
_____
_____

Family Adventure Time

Son, let's think about all the fantastic people who make up your family before we dive into these fun questions! Write their names here:
_____
_____

1. If each family member was a superhero, what would their superpowers be?
_____

2. If your family went on a big adventure or a trip, where would they go, and what would they do?
_____

3. The best thing about my family is...
_____

4. What's one tradition you have that makes your family unique?
_____

5. What's the funniest thing ever happening at one of the family dinners?
_____

Son, let's get creative! Draw your family as superheroes or in the middle of a big adventure. Maybe you're climbing a mountain, exploring space, or having a picnic with dragons! You can give each of them a cool outfit and superpowers.

Dad, now it's your turn to think about your family and answer these fun questions!

1. If each family member could turn into a mythical creature, what would they be and why?
   _____
   _____

2. The thing I admire most about my family is...
   _____

3. What family tradition do you want to start that you and your son can enjoy together every year?
   _____

4. If you had a family motto, what would it be?
   _____

5. What moment always makes you laugh when you think about it?
   _____
   _____

Dad, let's get creative too! Draw your family as mythical creatures in your favorite settings, such as a castle. Maybe one of your family is a wise dragon, another a clever fox, or a mythical goddess?

DIY Mini Twig Photo Frame Craft

Supplies You Need:
- Small twigs (gather from your yard or garden)
- Printed photo (sized to fit inside the frame)
- Scissors
- Twine or strong thread (for wrapping and securing the twigs and for hanging the frame)
- Glue (optionally)

Instructions:

1. Take the photo and cut the twigs to match the edges of your photo, leaving about 1 inch extra on each end for tying.

2. Lay the twigs in a square or rectangular shape around your photo. Optionally, for added stability, glue the twigs along the edges of the photo, placing them directly on the frame.

3. Tie the corners: Use twine or thread to tie the twigs together at each corner. Optionally, you can add extra twigs for a layered look. Wrap the twine around the crossing points of the twigs, knotting securely to hold the frame together.

4. Attach the photo: Use glue or punch small holes at the edges of the photo and use more twine to tie the photo to the frame. Alternatively, you can slide the photo behind the twigs and secure it with additional wraps of twine at each corner.

5. Add a hanging loop: Tie a piece of twine to the top corners of the frame to create a loop for hanging.

Brick Stamping Art

Get ready for a fun and creative art project using building bricks! This Brick Stamping Art activity is perfect for kids of all ages and a great way to spend an afternoon at home. Let's get started!

What You'll Need:
- Building Bricks: Use a variety of shapes and sizes for different stamp designs.
- Paint: Gouache or acrylic paint.
- Paper: Regular white paper or a large roll of paper for bigger projects.
- Felt (optional): A small piece to place under your paper for better stamping results.
- Optional: Extra paper to cover your work surface to protect it from paint.

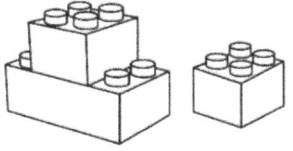

Instructions:
1. Gather Your Bricks:
   - Choose different sizes and shapes of building bricks for variety. Use flat plates for wider stamps and regular bricks for smaller, detailed prints.
2. Build Handles for Your Stamps:
   - Attach a few standard bricks on top of each flat plate or brick that you will use for stamping. This creates a handle, making it easier to press down without getting paint all over your fingers.
   - It is important to use the flat side of the brick for stamping!
3. Set Up Your Workspace:
   - Cover your table or work surface with extra paper to keep paint from getting on the table, making cleanup easier.
   - Place a piece of felt under the paper where you'll be stamping. The felt provides a little bit of cushion, which helps the brick stamps print clearly and evenly.
4. Start Stamping:
   - Slightly dip a brick into the paint, covering the bottom surface.
   - Firmly press the painted brick onto your paper to make a print. Experiment with different angles and pressing techniques to see how it changes the look of your stamp. Use different bricks to create various patterns and designs.
5. Get Creative:
   - Make different shapes and patterns, like houses, city skylines, robots, butterflies, or even spaceships! Arrange the bricks in whatever way your imagination suggests.

Tips:
- Use different colors of paint to make your designs more vibrant and interesting.
- Try overlapping stamps to create complex patterns.
- Experiment with how much pressure you use to see how it changes the appearance of the stamp.

Have fun and let your creativity run wild with Brick Stamping Art!

Nature Observers

Let's go outside and look for a bug that interests you. Be careful, and take your Dad with you, as some bugs can sting or cause allergies.

> Did you know?
>
> You can quickly and accurately identify unknown plants or bugs using technology. Choose a reputable plant or bug identification app and download it to your smartphone. Take a clear photo, ensuring you capture the whole plant or a detailed photo of a bug, and upload it to the app.

Find an ant, a butterfly, a beetle, or other insect. Watch the bug closely and observe its behavior.

Son, write the name of the bug:
_____

Notice if the bug is on a plant.

Dad, what plant is it?
_____

Son, how does the bug interact with the plant? Does it use the plant for food or shelter? Describe what you see in your journal.
_____
_____
_____

Sketch the Bug: Draw the bug you found and label its parts, such as the antennae, legs, wings, and other distinctive features. Imagine and draw a detailed picture of the bug's home. Include the plant and show how the bug uses it.

Exploring Animals in the Park or the Wild

Dad and Son, let's go to the park and look for an animal that interests you. Be careful and stay close to each other as you explore.

Look for animals in various places like trees, bushes, near water, or open fields.

Son, what animal did you find?

_____

What is it doing when you find it?

_____

Describe any sounds it makes or how it interacts with its environment.

_____

Son's Task: Draw a picture of the animal's tracks or traces in your journal.

Dad, describe these traces and explain what they tell you about the animal. Note the pattern in which the tracks are found. Are they in a straight line, zigzag, or in pairs? Describe how deep the tracks are. This can indicate the animal's weight and the type of ground.

_____
_____

Look for other traces like droppings, feathers, fur, nests, or burrows. Son, what did you find?

_____

Father-Son Indoor Scavenger Hunt

Dad and Son, let's explore your home to find items that reflect your unique relationship, personal traits, and shared experiences. Optionally, set a timer for an extra challenge and fun.

For Son to Find: What Son Found

Dad's favorite snack _____ ☐

An object that represents Dad's favorite way to relax on his own _____ ☐

An item that represents Dad's favorite type of music or song _____ ☐

Something that reminds you of a trip or adventure you had with Dad _____ ☐

An item that matches the color of Dad's eyes _____ ☐

A picture or object that reminds you of a fun memory with Dad _____ ☐

An item that reminds you of something Dad has taught you _____ ☐

Dad, what do you think about Son's choices? _____

For Dad to Find:	What Son Found	
An item that represents Son's favorite color	_____	☐
Your favorite gift from Son	_____	☐
An item that represents Son's unique way of thinking	_____	☐
Something that reminds you of an accomplishment Son achieved	_____	☐
An item that represents Son's favorite time of year	_____	☐
An object that reminds you of a special bonding moment with Son	_____	☐

Son, what do you think of Dad's choices? _____
_____
_____

Personality Iceberg

Dad and Son

Imagine your personality as a giant iceberg floating in the ocean. Like a real iceberg, only a small part is visible above the water, while most is hidden below the surface.

- **The Tip of the Iceberg:** This is what people you don't know well see. It's like the first impression you give when you meet someone new. Examples: Quiet, Shy, Friendly, Outgoing.
- **Below the Surface:** This is the part of you that only your closest friends and family know. It's where your true self shines with all your amazing qualities. Examples: Creative, Kind, Funny, Curious.

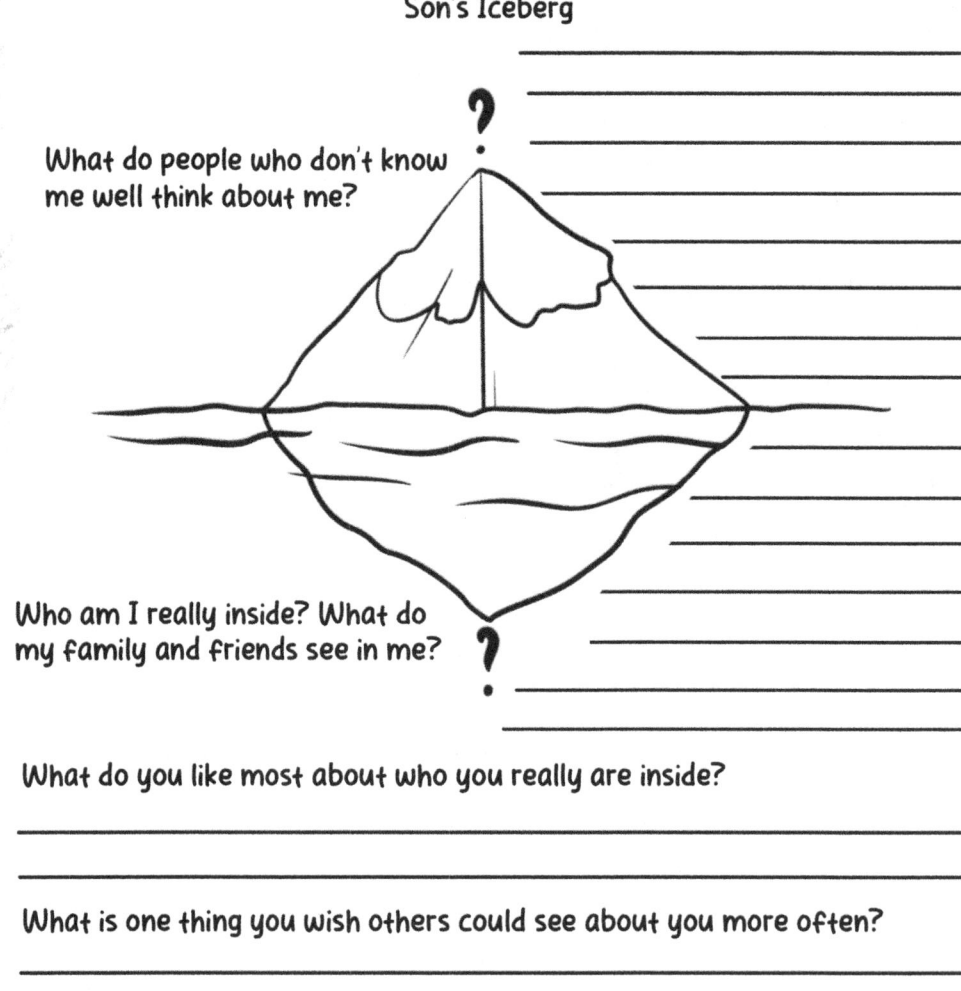

Son's Iceberg

What do people who don't know me well think about me?

Who am I really inside? What do my family and friends see in me?

What do you like most about who you really are inside?
_____
_____

What is one thing you wish others could see about you more often?
_____
_____

Dad's Iceberg

What do people who don't know me well think about me?

_____
_____
_____
_____
_____
_____
_____
_____

Who am I really inside? What do my family and friends see in me?

_____
_____
_____

What do you like most about who you really are inside?
_____
_____

What is one thing you wish others could see about you more often?
_____
_____

Opposites Day Adventure

Explore and appreciate each other's interests by swapping roles!

Son, choose a cool activity you enjoy and write it on the list or use activities in the example. Write down tasks for your Dad to complete during each activity. For each completed task, color in a star. Compete with your Dad to see who can complete the most tasks! Examples:
- Challenge Dad to build a building constructor creation alongside you. See whose creation is the tallest, most creative, or follows a specific theme.
- Set up a mini race track using toys or objects around the house. Instruct Dad to race with you, keeping track of who wins each round.
- Guide Dad through a day as a robot! Give him funny instructions to follow, like walking in slow motion or speaking in a robot voice while doing tasks.
- Instruct Dad to create a new invention using items around the house, such as a robot, gadget, or creative contraption.

List:

Tasks for Dad:

_____   _____ ☆

_____   _____ ☆

_____   _____ ☆

_____   _____ ☆

_____   _____ ☆

_____   _____ ☆

_____   _____ ☆

_____   _____ ☆

_____   _____ ☆

Dad, choose an activity you enjoy and write it on the list. Write down tasks for your Son to complete during each activity. For each completed task, color in a star. Compete with your Son to see who can complete the most tasks! Examples:

- Teach your Son how to use basic tools. Build something together, like a birdhouse or a small project.
- Show your Son how to set up a tent, tie knots, or use a compass. Take him on a short hike or adventure walk.
- Introduce your Son to a sport or activity you enjoy. Teach him how to throw a ball, dribble, or swing, and have a mini-tournament!
- Teach your Son how to cast a line and talk about different types of bait. Enjoy fishing together and share tips.

List:

Tasks for Son:

_____

_____

_____

_____

_____

_____

_____

_____

_____

_____

Count how many stars each of you has colored. Celebrate your achievements and enjoy a small treat or reward together!

FINISHING THE JOURNAL!

Date: _____

Dad and Son,
You've made it to the end! Be proud of the work that you did exploring your special bond! What do you think about your journey through this book? Did you have fun?

_____
_____
_____
_____

What was your favorite part?

_____
_____
_____
_____

What should you do after this book? Write your ideas!

_____
_____

LET'S SEAL THE ENVELOPE!

Son, let's seal the Time Capsule envelope by creating a cute wax seal. Be careful and let your Dad complete the steps with the hot wax and flame. Here's how to do it:

Materials Needed
- Wax or crayons. If you're using crayons, remove the paper wrapping.
- Thread or Thin Ribbon.
- Metal Button with an interesting design. This will be used as your stamp.
- Heat Source: A lighter, matches, or a candle.
- Spoon or Metal Ladle: To melt the wax in.

Steps to Create a Wax Seal

1. Prepare Your Workspace.

2. Melt the Wax: Break the wax or crayons into small pieces and place them in the spoon or ladle. Hold the spoon over the flame until the wax melts completely.

3. Pour the Wax: Carefully pour the melted wax onto the envelope or paper where you want your seal. Pour enough to create a small pool about the size of a coin.

4. Place the Thread: Lay one end of the thread into the pool of wax, letting it trail off the edge of the envelope.

5. Wait a few seconds after pouring the wax for it to cool slightly, then press your button or coin firmly into the wax.

6. Leave the button or coin in place for about 30 seconds to a minute. Gently peel the button or coin away from the wax.

Most importantly, write the date when you sealed the envelope and when it is allowed to be opened!

Made in the USA
Las Vegas, NV
30 January 2025

17226299R00056